Interactive Learning in the Higher Education Classroom

Cooperative, Collaborative, and Active Learning Strategies

Harvey C. Foyle
Editor

Excellence in the Academy
the nea **professional library** *higher education series*
National Education Association
Washington, D.C.

Printing History
First Printing: May 1995

Note
The opinions expressed in this publication should not be construed as representing the policy or position of the National Education Association. Materials published by the NEA Professional Library are intended to be discussion documents for educators who are concerned with specialized interests of the profession.

This book is printed on acid-free paper.   This book is printed with soy ink.

ACID FREE
∞

Library of Congress Cataloging-in-Publication Data
Interactive learning in the higher education classroom/
     Harvey C. Foyle, editor.
     p. cm.—
     "The NEA professional library higher education series."
     Includes bibliographical references.
     ISBN 0-8106-2679

ACKNOWLEDGMENTS

I would like to thank the administration, faculty, and staff of Emporia State University, especially The Teachers College, for providing an atmosphere of collegiality and support in a cooperative, collaborative, and active learning environment.

A special thank you goes to Timothy Crawford, NEA Professional Library, for his encouragement and support for our writing efforts. In addition, acknowledgment must go to Lawrence Lyman for his creative thoughts and guidance over the years.

Groucho Marx once quipped, "Outside of a dog, a book is man's best friend. Inside of a dog, it's too dark to read." Thank you goes to my many students who have provided light on this subject. I hope this book becomes someone's best friend.

Harvey C. Foyle
Editor

The Editor

Harvey C. Foyle (Ph.D., Kansas State University, 1984) is Associate Professor in The Teachers College, Emporia State University, Emporia, Kansas.

The Advisory Panel

Lyn Le Countryman
Assistant Professor of Teaching and Science Education
University of Northern Iowa
Cedar Falls, Iowa

David J. León
Professor of Ethnic Studies
California State University
Sacramento, California

Jim Wilson
Professor of Speech Communication
Broward Community College
Ft. Lauderdale, Florida

CONTENTS

PREFACE

Higher education faculty, or for that matter, post-secondary instructors, are shifting their instructional methods in order to meet the changes in the public schools and the changes in society as a whole. Students are leaving the public schools with experiences that involve them with their own education. Thus, instructors are using more strategies that involve collaborative, cooperative, and active learning approaches.

This book has four sections. Part I, The Rationale for Change, provides the "why" or need for changing from traditional instructional methods to methods that involve more student collaboration with the instructor. Part II, Applications, specifies collaborative methods as examples in specific courses. Part III, Assessment, supplies practical methods and forms for evaluating group work. Part IV, Off to a Good Start, furnishes instructors with ready-to-use collaborative strategies that can be used immediately by both novice and experienced faculty.

Cooperative Learning is now a well-defined methodology and is, therefore, capitalized whenever the term is used in this book. Collaborative and active learning are less formalized and not tied to specific strategies as much as Cooperative Learning is. Indeed, for the most part, collaborative learning involves students in working with one another. Active learning may involve students in working together or may involve active interaction between the student and the teacher.

The writers in this book use student interactive strategies in their classrooms and, thus, are well-experienced to provide insights into collaborative student instruction. Faculty in The Teachers College of Emporia State University are highly represented in this work. In fact, The Teachers College has won numerous national awards in education and these faculty have received awards in instruction, scholarly activity, and service.

The editor would like to thank all of the writers of this book. They put forth a great deal of effort to share their ideas and strategies with others. As a great teacher (Luke 6:40) once said, "A disciple is not above His teacher, but every one when he is fully taught will be like his teacher." The strategies presented in this book will help students become like their teachers in their search for knowledge.

PART I

THE RATIONALE FOR CHANGE

Higher education faculty members usually see their roles as that of information givers and skill builders. To fulfill these roles, instructors use multiple methods for providing the information and building the skills. Variations of the traditional lecture-discussion method are widely used in many academic settings. In recent years, instructors have been turning to more interactive learning approaches in order to stimulate student thinking, motivate student involvement, and enhance student learning.

David C. Foyle and Michael G. Shafto point out the need for cooperation and collaboration in higher education classrooms. They believe that students should be prepared to work in groups and to work on team projects in order to enhance their involvement in work groups and team projects in government and industry. These NASA research scientists have found that team work must not just be talked about but must be implemented in order to fulfill NASA's goals. They point out the contradictions of team work and individual work with an emphasis on teamwork.

Laura M. Ventimiglia, building upon her experience as an adjunct faculty member and a community college instructor, provides us with the fundamentals of Cooperative Learning and promotes the concept of collaboration in the classroom.

Bill Yates provides us with the rationale for using the computer for problem solving with collaborative groups of students. Indeed, problem-solving skills are integral to higher education courses and can be enhanced by using technology

9

in cooperative groups.

This section suggests that students who work in groups in post-secondary classrooms will be better prepared to work in teams on group problem-solving projects after they leave the classroom and enter the world of work.

1

TEAMWORK IN THE REAL WORLD

by David C. Foyle and Michael G. Shafto

The National Aeronautics and Space Administration (NASA) is well known for its roles in the space program and in aeronautics. Because teamwork is essential for most NASA missions, NASA has experience in both research on teamwork and implementation of team projects.

For example, a single Orbiter (space shuttle) mission requires a large team of people, well into the thousands, working toward the common goal of launch, mission deployment, and recovery. This large team is actually composed of separate smaller teams: the launch team at Kennedy Space Center near Cape Canaveral, Florida; the Mission Control (mission planning and communications) team at Johnson Space Center in Houston, Texas; and the Orbiter landing/processing team at Dryden Flight Research Center in Edwards, California.

Likewise, in aeronautics there are projects composed of smaller groups of people organized around disciplines, all working toward the same goal. One example is the High-Speed Civil Transport Program, aimed at designing a supersonic aircraft for the year 2005 (America's second-generation Concorde). This project involves teams from several NASA centers and industry. Formal research in the area of teamwork has also been underway at NASA since the late 1970s (Chambers & Nagel, 1985; Rouse & Lauber, 1984; Wiener & Curry, 1980; Wiener & Nagel, 1988). The cockpit crew of today's airliners is a team, and is officially viewed as such by many airlines. Airlines train crews as teams and have them work in these teams during actual line operation. NASA's research into this area has shown that teamwork, as demonstrated in crew communication style, is important for safe, smooth, and efficient aircraft operation (Wiener, Kanki, & Helmreich, 1993).

The purpose of this chapter is not to summarize research results on teamwork. (For a review of research, see

McGrath & Altman, 1966; Hare,1976; Latham,1988; or Klein, Orasanu, Calderwood, & Zsambok, 1993.) This chapter will summarize our insight into teamwork as it applies to the large institutions and organizations with which we have been associated: university academic systems, Navy research laboratories, and NASA. These organizations represent a variety of systems in which teamwork is commonplace.

Problem: The Individual versus The Team

There is a natural tension that occurs in teams when team goals and individual goals conflict. Smith and Berg (1987) refer to this as the "paradox of identity." The team typically is defined around a specific project or product, and is aimed at completing that project or developing that specific product. The individual works toward that goal as well, but has specific, uniquely individual subgoals related to the development and use of his or her own technical expertise.

One example that we have seen in our experience is that of software development. A few years ago at a NASA center, there was a large project aimed at developing an advanced software system to monitor a control unit for a new aerospace system. The programmers were all intelligent and capable; in fact, maybe too much so. Rather than spending time generating the computer code to carry out the system monitoring, team members were more interested in developing new ways of conceptualizing the underlying technical problems. In other words, they were more interested in developing their own understanding of a variety of advanced software methodologies than in applying the current state of the art to finishing the project. They were playing a project game by research rules, or speaking "research-ese" in a country full of "project-ese" speakers.

When they reached an impasse with those new concepts, the programmers would take a detour and pursue another new and interesting concept. Additionally, the programmers spent time building special tools and languages to aid in the development of the project software, rather than doing the actual coding and testing necessary to complete the project.

Curtis, Krasner, and Iscoe (1988) analyzed a number of large software projects and found that one of the main reasons for project failure was the lack of a consistent, integrated framework for communication among team members. Individuals working alone have little need for such a framework, but when a team is pursuing a well-defined project goal, all the team members need to be speaking the same language. This requires a careful, disciplined approach. Think what would happen on a football team if each player wrote his own playbook!

Constantine (1993, p. 104) points out that "cowboys have been known to gather not only at rodeos and roundups, but at large software houses, where they create complex system software." This "cowboy" approach toward a project is the expression of the team member's need for professional development and recognition. Such individual needs are legitimate, but in a team project they must be subordinated to the team's needs.

Problem: Reward Structures

There is typically a difference between what employers say they want and what they reward. Reward structures (salary increases, bonuses, promotions) typically reward individual achievements, rather than contributions to group goals, although teams may also receive recognition and rewards (such as group recognition and/or monetary awards). Recognition as an important team member arises only to the extent that the individual is seen as valuable, and his or her specific contributions are viewed as excellent. The tension that exists between the individual and the team is expressed as the individual's demonstrating his or her unique value, while the team requires integrated group behaviors that bring the team closer to its goal. Software engineers use the term egoless programming to mean the opposite of the "cowboy" approach.

In academia, as well as in industry and in government laboratories, administrators see teamwork as an important way to integrate disciplines. One new interdisciplinary program that has emerged at universities is Cognitive Science. Cognitive Science studies the wide range of areas related to human cognition (memory, thinking, language, learning, and decision making). Typically, the departments that form the program include some subset of psychology, computer science, linguistics, neuroscience, and philosophy. Usually faculty members from these departments form a team to oversee the interdisciplinary Cognitive Science program.

The success of Cognitive Science and similar programs is somewhat checkered. Students involved in the interdisciplinary program can have the problem of being caught in the middle, because no department feels a strong sense of "ownership" of the student. Graduate students may be required to meet all the requirements of all the departments involved — not an interdisciplinary approach, but a multidisciplinary one! This effectively penalizes the students in the program and undermines the program's success. Similarly, we are aware of faculty members in psychology departments that were advised to stop collaborations with Computer Science faculty members (in spite of the interdisciplinary nature of Cognitive Science), for exactly the same reasons: The faculty member was viewed as "not doing psychology" and in fact was advised that he was putting his tenure in jeopardy. He was told outright that interdisciplinary publications would not count toward building his case for tenure.

The reward structures in the university systems and government laboratories are very clear, due to the large size of the organizations, and the need for objectivity. For tenure or promotion at a research university, such things as teaching ability and committee membership are weighed as a small percentage with the greatest weighting for one's research publication record. Acting as sole author on a paper is worth the most, first author on papers with two authors is worth somewhat less, second author on papers with two authors is worth even less, and so on. Clearly, in this reward system, teamwork is acknowledged as having some value, but not as much as working alone. Similar promotion criteria are used in the government laboratories. Mixed messages are being sent to the researchers/professors when they are told to work on interdisciplinary teams, or project teams, but the reward structure is clearly biased against that teamwork.

Problem: Hierarchies and Teamwork

Simon (1981) pointed out that large organizations (universities, research laboratories, corporations) tend to organize themselves into a hierarchical structure. There are problems associated with hierarchies, including such things as inflexibility due to bureaucracy, slow response due to compartmentalization, and (most important) lack of communication within and among different levels of the hierarchy. As one goes upward in the hierarchy in the direction of the corporate president, one has an increasing amount of authority and responsibility accompanied by a decreasing amount of relevant knowledge. In the extreme, senior managers may not have adequate information and may be "out-of-the-loop," yet they are still making crucial decisions. Teamwork may be a solution to these inherent problems within hierarchically structured organizations. Teams can work across the hierarchical structure, effectively bridging the gaps and boundaries that are found (Deming, 1993).

THE NASA TAP PROGRAM: A TEAM OF TEAMS

Teamwork becomes necessary when a problem or project is too large to be solved by a single person. One such program is NASA's Terminal Area Productivity (TAP) program. It is a large program aimed at increasing the operational capacity of U.S. airports (see Rouse & Lauber, 1984). The TAP program is a multimillion dollar, multiyear program spanning two NASA centers, other government laboratories, and many aerospace companies.

Teamwork on such a large program operates on multiple levels. At the lowest level, the day-to-day working level, there are many small teams of 2 to 10 people working to design or evaluate concepts or subsystems being developed for the TAP program. For example, at NASA Ames Research Center in California, the first author is working with two other researchers and a computer graphics programmer to develop a display using superimposed symbology to aid the pilots in taxiing the aircraft from the runway to the gate under low-visibility weather conditions. For the TAP program, the "Superimposed Symbology for Taxi" team is responsible only for that particular display design, and only during the taxi phase of operation. This team functions as one might expect, with informal hallway discussions about display issues and ideas, as well as "round table" meetings and formal reviews in which various ideas and plans are critiqued. In this case, the team members all have offices in the same building, and all have worked together on various other projects over the past few years.

Also, at NASA Ames Research Center, other similarly structured teams are working on moving plan-view maps for taxis, the detection of runway obstacles, and systems to help air traffic controllers. At Langley Research Center in Virginia, other teams are developing displays for landing (as opposed to taxiing) in low-visibility conditions and are evaluating in-flight hardware systems and display formats. The airframe manufacturers and avionics companies are also working on various aspects of the TAP program.

Within the TAP program, there are the day-to-day working level teams (such as the "Superimposed Symbology for Taxi" team). That team also works with other working-level teams. One such example is that the "Superimposed Symbology for Taxi" team is planning a joint evaluation with the "Moving Map for Taxi" team, in which the interactions of both displays will be evaluated. Essentially, these two teams now form a "team of teams," or a new team: the "Taxi Display" team. As one moves upward in the TAP program hierarchy, other teams emerge. In the next few years, the "Taxi Display" team from NASA Ames Research Center in California will be working with the "Flight Test Evaluation" team from NASA Langley Research Center in Virginia to conduct evaluations of the displays in-flight on board a Boeing 757 aircraft.

Teamwork Is Real

Teamwork in the real world is real. There are problems associated with teamwork, mostly related to evaluation, but teams are an effective way to parse large problems into manageable ones. As one can see, teamwork at NASA includes many different levels of teams: Many small teams work on a particular portion of a program, with these teams working together at various stages of the program, and those new "teams of teams" working with other "teams of teams." Teams are important in space mission operations (Connors, Harrison, & Akins 1985), in aeronautical research (Wiener et al., 1993), and in advanced software development (Curtis et al., 1988).

All teams face similar problems: Individual goals must be harmonized with team goals. A reward structure must be devised that recognizes the value of teamwork, as well as the value of individual creativity and excellence. Interdisciplinary skills must be put on an equal footing with narrowly channeled expertise. Focused attention must be given to the establishment and maintenance of a common framework and language for communication among team members. Teams must be designed to promote communication and cooperation across organizational boundaries and among different hierarchical levels. The potential payoffs for effective teamwork include reductions in the time and cost required for project completion. The most exciting payoff, however, is the ability of the team to achieve goals that the individual team members could not meet alone. This has been NASA's guiding principle since the early days of the Apollo Project.

REFERENCES

Chambers, A. B., & Nagel, D. C. (1985). Pilots of the future: Human or computer? *Communications of the Association for Computing Machinery* 28: 1187-1199.

Connors, M. M., Harrison, A. A., & Akins, F. R. (1985). *Living Aloft: Human Requirements for Extended Space Flight*. Washington, DC: NASA Scientific and Technical Information Branch.

Constantine, L. L. (1993, October). Cowboy homecoming. *Software Development* 104.

Curtis, B., Krasner, H., & Iscoe, N. (1988). A field study of the software design process for large systems. *Communications of the Association for Computing Machinery* 31: 1268-1287.

Deming, W. E. (1993). *The New Economics for Industry, Government, Education*. Cambridge, MA: MIT Center for Advanced Engineering Study.

Hare, P. A. (1976). *Handbook of Small Group Research*. 2d. ed. New York: Free Press.

Klein, G. A., Orasanu, J. M., Calderwood, R., & Zsambok, C. E. eds. (1993). *Decision Making in Action: Models and Methods*. Norwood, NJ: Ablex.

Latham, G. P. (1988). Human resource training and development. *Annual Review of Psychology* 39: 545-82.

McGrath, J. E., & Altman, I. (1966). *Small Group Research*. New York: Holt, Rinehart and Winston.

Rouse, W. B., & Lauber, J. K. (1984). Report of the Panel on Human Factors. In *Aeronautics Technology Possibilities for 2000: Report of a Workshop*. Washington, DC: National Research Council, Commission on Engineering and Technical Systems, Aeronautics and Space Engineering Board.

Simon, H. A. (1981). *The Sciences of the Artificial*. 2d ed. Cambridge, MA: MIT Press.

Smith, K. K., & Berg, D .N. (1987). A paradoxical conception of group dynamics. *Human Relations* 40: 633-58.

Wiener, E. L., & Curry, R. E. (1980). Flight-deck automation: Promises and problems. *Ergonomics* 23: 995-1011.

Wiener, E. L., & Nagel, D. C. eds. (1988). *Human Factors in Aviation*. New York: Academic Press.

Wiener, E. L., Kanki, B. G., & Helmreich, R. L. eds. (1993). *Cockpit Resource Management*. New York: Academic Press.

2

COOPERATIVE LEARNING
AT THE COLLEGE LEVEL

by Laura M. Ventimiglia

Professors where I teach have shown, in both introductory and upper-level courses in the disciplines of history,
political science, English, math, and chemistry, that cooperation and collaboration are effective teaching and learning
strategies. In fact, whole programs at these colleges—Writing
Across the Curriculum, Freshman Seminar, and many others—
are built around these concepts. Faced with the responsibility
of providing students with new skills for new times, faculty
are initiating cooperative experiences in their classrooms and
in their own practice with colleagues. Their cooperative and
collaborative teaching and learning strategies also have the
advantage of improving student learning and retention. The
research on cooperative learning shows an increase in student
achievement (Slavin 1989/90[1]; Johnson, Johnson, and Smith
1991a, 1991b). Research also indicates that meaningful learning—learning that connects new information to existing cognitive structures of an individual—is more effective (Johnson,
1975).

The shift from a professor-centered to a student-cen-
tered learning situation allows students to construct new
knowledge by building on existing schema. Students also
share in the ownership of course content, making it more
meaningful and useful. The role of professor is transformed
from one of deliverer-of-information to one of colleague and
mentor. Belenky, Clinchy, Goldberger, and Tarule (1986) refer
to this role as one of a midwife. Midwife professors "assist. . .
students in giving birth to their own ideas, in making their

This material was modified and reprinted from Ventimiglia, L. M. (Winter
1994). Cooperative learning at the college level. *Thought & Action* IX
(2): 5-30.

own tacit knowledge explicit and elaborating on it" (p. 217). Freire (1970) and Sizer (1984, 1992) support this approach to education with their descriptions of educators as co-investigators and coaches.

The methodology of cooperative and collaborative teaching is also important because of the skills students develop from this process approach to education. The two skills we will all need to be successful in the workforce 2000—neither of which is taught as the content of a course or from a textbook—are the ability to work together cooperatively and the ability to be a lifelong learner. Industrial/organizational psychologists point out that in our fast-changing society, people will need to change or relearn their careers eight to 13 times during their life span (Schultz & Schultz, 1990).

Both cooperative and collaborative learning, in any discipline, give students the opportunity to learn these skills by completing the course as designed and by imitating the academic behaviors modeled by the professor. In the cooperative and collaborative learning patterns, we model our actual work processes—students can see us struggling to solve a problem, interpreting a primary source, or revising a paper.

Different Models to Education

The traditional approach to education, described as the banking model by Freire (1970), has been the lecture format where information is "deposited" into students. The professor, one who considers himself knowledgeable, dictates both the form and content of course requirements by bestowing on those he considers to know nothing, the students, the information that he determines is appropriate for them and society. Freire points out that, in this model, students are expected to adapt to their world, not transform it, by passively receiving this information.

Tompkins (1990) describes another, more contemporary approach called the performance model. Even though students may become more involved in the process of their own education by choosing their own topics for research papers and by suggesting topics and readings for class discussion, Tompkins suggests that professors are basically concerned, as she was, with how well they perform in the classroom. A professor who teaches under the performance model generally wants to show students how smart he or she is, how knowledgeable, and how well-prepared he or she is for class.

I would like to suggest yet another approach to education: the collaborative model. The collaborative model builds on Cooperative Learning strategies but extends beyond having the students work together to complete a predetermined task. In collaborative learning, professors and students actively and mutually engage in the learning process. Together, they define and create a body of knowledge that informs and transforms our world. In this approach to education, professors are, in fact, midwives, co-investigators, coaches, who together with their students construct the knowledge for the course.

As a psychology professor at both a community college and a comprehensive liberal arts state college, I want my students to be empowered to change the world in which we live. To do this, they need to learn to use their minds well while critically learning the content of the course. They need to learn to respect themselves and respect others. Cooperative and collaborative strategies accomplish this and, at the same time, develop a culture for quality work.

As mentioned above, cooperative and collaborative techniques are not particular to any one discipline. Faculty seem committed to the concept of cooperative and collaborative learning, but many do not understand that success at these approaches is grounded in the structure designed by the professor. Using cooperative and collaborative techniques requires a tremendous amount of work before, during, and after actual class time.

COOPERATIVE AND COLLABORATIVE TECHNIQUES
Past and Present

During my first semester of teaching, I structured my classes to actively engage students in the learning process. Students generally came to class excited and ready to learn, but something was missing. I realized that students evaluated themselves and others according to "intellectual abilities." Those who were "smart," who stayed focused on the task at hand, who gave reasonable answers, and who spoke quickly and clearly, were valuable. Those who were less focused, less accurate, and had trouble speaking were worthless, and in some cases not even tolerated. Students openly made derogatory comments and inappropriate facial expressions toward other students. In addition, the expectancy rule was in effect. Students responded to fellow students' expectations and behaved in the fashion in which they were perceived. Students who were smart by their peers' standards continued to perform well in class, and students who were less acceptable, performed poorly.

I could see the strengths and weaknesses of every student within my classes I could see that each student had something worth valuing. But they couldn't see this value in each other; sometimes they couldn't even see this value in themselves. As the professor, I observed their behaviors in the classroom, read their academic journals, and talked to them individually. I was, therefore, exposed to their work, their thoughts, their feelings. I could appreciate and recognize the contribution each student could make to society. Since my goals were to encourage students to learn and respect themselves and others, I would need to find a way to provide knowledge of self and others to all students. I was sure this would raise the level of respect as students came to know each other and see in each person something worth valuing. My initiation of Cooperative Learning in the classroom, therefore, stemmed from the educational shortcomings of my own classes—the absence of a mutual respect that included an appreciation for each other's contribution to society.

At the conclusion of my first semester of teaching, I determined that the second semester would be different. I turned to the literature on Cooperative Learning and found three common areas of concern: group formation, group composition, and assessment of student work. Using that information, I began experimenting with Cooperative Learning groups.[2]

Group Formation

Group formation refers to the number of students in each group, the assignment of students to each group, and the length of time groups stay together. Aronson, Blaney, Stephan, Sikes, and Snapp (1978) believe that groups can consist of three to seven members, with five to six being the ideal. Johnson, Johnson, and Smith (1991a, 1991b) suggest that groups consist of two to four members. They further suggest that the professor assign students to groups or use random assignment. They recommend that if students select their own group members, a modified student selection process be used. Students may list the people they want to work with, but the professor arranges groups so that students are placed in a group with one person they have selected and others that the professor has selected. Groups should stay together long enough for students to be productive, but every student in the class should have the opportunity to work with every other student sometime during the semester.

For several semesters, students in my courses were assigned to groups either randomly or by matching people according to abilities, both intellectual and interpersonal. During other semesters, students assigned themselves either by choosing a topic or by choosing the students with whom they wanted to work. The size of groups in my classes has always ranged from three to five students and, presently, I use a variety of assignment methods during one semester. I begin the semester by allowing students to choose their own group members for work that is introductory to course content. During the second or third week, I begin using random assignment.

Depending on classroom dynamics, students work together to complete one, two, or more tasks, work that is topical in content. For example, students may stay in the same group to complete assignments related to families and gender roles or learning and memory, but then group membership would change for the next topic or topics. I strive to complete a series of assignments for two topics, but often find it counterproductive to remain focused on the selection process of the group and not the needs of the class.

One semester, for example, students in one developmental psychology course worked well when assigned to groups randomly and completed two sets of topical tasks. Yet students in another developmental psychology course were not productive using that same design. In the second case, students had the opportunity of working with every other classmate via random assignment for the completion of one set of tasks. They worked the rest of the semester in stable groups and with members of their choosing. Producing quality work is my expectation of students, but often students cannot develop—in one semester—the skills needed to work productively with a range of other people.

GROUP COMPOSITION

I also pay attention to *group composition*. Group composition refers to the makeup of the group in terms of skill levels, gender, race, and personality traits. Both Aronson et al. (1978) and Johnson, Johnson, and Smith (1991a, 1991b) believe that a diverse group membership is most productive. During the semesters that I assigned students to groups by matching abilities, I observed the productiveness of diverse skill levels and personalities within each group.

I found that matching students by intellectual and interpersonal abilities drew more attention to those areas of strengths and weaknesses in students and was ineffective. I tried, for instance, to arrange group membership so that the number of male and female students were balanced, or groups were either predominately male or female, or were all male or female. I found that individual student characteristics were more influential than gender in producing quality work. I am only now becoming aware of the impact of ethnic diversity within group membership. I am observing students in intraracial as well as interracial groups.

I rely on random assignment to produce effective group membership, but I will interfere with the process occasionally. If random assignment hasn't brought people together who may benefit from working with each other, I will arrange groups for that purpose. Or if I notice that unhealthy dynamics are interfering with a group's productiveness, I may also arrange groups.

Assessment of Student Work

This area seems to produce the most confusion among my colleagues. It is no wonder, given the range of descriptions one finds in the literature. Johnson, Johnson, and Smith (1991a, 1991b) believe in individual accountability. Students are held responsible for learning the material themselves and then helping others learn.

Aronson et al. (1978) believe in individual testing. Kagan (1989/90; cited in Brandt, 1989/90) and Slavin (1989/90) discuss the benefits of group goals and individual accountability. Group goals or positive interdependence require group members to work together for rewards based on group success. One measure of group success could be the total of individual group members' test scores. McDougall and Gimple (1985) also refer to group rewards. But Jackson (1986) refers to group grades. The discussion here raises the question of individual versus group grades for the novice cooperative learning professor. And, does the type of work students do influence whether they receive an individual or group grade? To help answer these questions, I have also experimented with the type of work done by each group and the evaluation of that work.

Group work has included class presentations, group tests, applying concepts to a given situation, and group-to-group presentations. Assessment of student work has included grades that were based on an individual's work and grades that were based on the group's work. Students in my introductory psychology courses, for example, have worked in groups both in and out of class to prepare a class presentation on a psychological disorder. The assignment remained the same for three semesters, but the grading changed from an individual grade, to a group grade, to a combination of both.

Presently, students receive only individual grades for the work they do in my courses. Some students are not able to commit to group work on a consistent basis and in such a way that would make group grades equitable. These students are either incapable of such total commitment or their personal lives interfere with the responsibilities of being a student. It is not uncommon for students to be called away from their school work because of their own job commitments, family responsibilities, or personal dilemmas.

In all my classes, however, course requirements are built on interdependence and individual accountability. Class participation grades are based on attendance, individual preparedness, and the degree of cooperation, which includes helping others learn the material for the course. Journal work is a record of the individual's learning process, but it is enhanced by the work of classmates. Final exams in developmental psychology courses are comprehensive and reflect the work of the entire class throughout the semester. Final exams in introductory psychology courses are self-evaluative but include an assessment of the student's ability to work with others. Individual competency is achieved, therefore, through cooperation and collaboration.

The type of work done by groups in my classes depends on the type of group to which students belong. There are now two types of groups in my classes: cooperative learning groups and collaborative learning groups. I often hear colleagues use these terms interchangeably, but I recognize two very major distinctions in the type of work each group does and the resources each group uses.

COOPERATIVE LEARNING GROUPS

Cooperative Learning groups take their direction from and use sources provided by the professor. Because I recognize cooperative work as a precursor to collaborative work, students in my introductory level courses are exposed to cooperative group work.

From Theory to Practice

The direction takes the form of established questions to direct student discussions and established activities that require students to apply concepts. Sources include only the textbook or materials prepared by the professor. For example, before a lecture on psychobiological processes, students are presented with the question: Do you believe psychologists should be concerned with the nervous system?

Students are expected to justify their position and be specific in their rationale. They prepare for their small group discussions before class by critically reading their textbooks and developing their own arguments. They bring those arguments to class and, using each person's work, they develop a group position to present to the class. These presentations become the basis for the class lecture and discussion.

Taking Notes

The natural response of students in classrooms not cooperatively based is to take notes only when the professor speaks and outlines salient points. In my classes, students are instructed to take notes when each student presents but to leave plenty of "white space" in their notebooks. I take notes as well, recording mine on the blackboard. The white space in student notebooks is later filled with additional points, clarifications, or implications derived from the whole class discussion.

Students take peer presentations very seriously. They are told from the beginning of the semester that what anyone says in class is as important as what I say. If they aren't quite convinced, they realize this soon enough when I do not repeat what students have presented, yet hold the class accountable for that information through testing.

Lectures

Cooperative Learning groups may also function after a lecture. Following a lecture on classical conditioning, students are given the group task of identifying the elements of classical conditioning in a variety of situations presented to them on an activity sheet. For example, students are asked to identify the neutral stimulus (ns), unconditioned stimulus (ucs), unconditioned response (ucr), conditioned stimulus (cs), and conditioned response (cr) in the following situation:

> Two-year-old Andrew is in his playpen in front of a big picture window. A thunder and lightning storm is brewing outside. A bolt of lightning flashes across the window, followed by a loud thunder clap. Andrew jumps at the noise. This continues for quite some time and then stops. As the storm moves away, a bolt of lightning flashes again. Andrew sees the flash and jumps.

Students quickly move into groups perceiving this as a fun activity. They are surprised at how difficult it is to actually apply the information they have just heard in the lecture. Within the group, though, they arrive at the solution:

ns = lightning, ucs = thunderclap, ucr = jump,
cs = lightning, cr = jump.

Cooperative Learning classes take their direction and receive sources from the professor, as opposed to collaborative learning groups, which provide their own direction and sources. These students are working on a higher cognitive level.

COLLABORATIVE LEARNING GROUPS
Students Set the Topics

Students in my developmental psychology classes work collaboratively and begin initially by setting the priority for topics to be covered during the semester. During the first class, each student is given 100 points to spend before the next class. Using the table of contents in their textbook, they assign points to those topics they wish to study. I compile the results and give students the course outline and reading assignments at the third class. As each topic comes up in class, students work in small groups brainstorming questions they have about the topic. Each group develops at least three questions that are then written on the blackboard. In an adulthood and old age class, for example, a group raised the following questions under the topic of families:

- Do children of divorced parents tend to get divorced themselves?

- What are the effects on children reared in gay or lesbian families?
- In choosing a mate, is it better to pick one who is similar or opposite?
- Do people consciously or unconsciously choose someone who is similar to or different from their opposite sex parent?
- Do couples who marry later in life and get to know each other before the marriage stay married longer than couples who marry young?

Once students have listed the group questions on the board, we categorize them. These questions, along with questions from the other groups in class, were categorized into:
- choosing a mate,
- marriage,
- gay and lesbian relationships, and
- marriage and divorce.

Each group then chooses a category to investigate and which questions will direct the group's work. Students work with their small groups to prepare for the whole class discussion on each topic. Preparation involves planning the coverage of the topic, developing strategies for each group member's work, researching a variety of sources, and putting together a presentation for the whole class discussion.

Resources

Sources include scholarly journal articles, textbook readings, and monographs. Media stories or pamphlets from legitimate agencies such as pamphlets on menopause or child abuse may be used to provide examples in support of group findings. Periodicals such as *Psychology Today, Newsweek,* or *Time* are not considered scholarly sources.

The textbook is treated as a resource and not a definitive text. Students use their textbook for its index to look for information that they can read or access on their chosen topic. The value of using a textbook as a resource is that students learn to think for themselves and understand that textbooks usually represent a singular point of view. I work right along with my students. I choose a topic to investigate, do research in the library, and present my findings to the class. I work with students in and out of class, although my out-of-class sessions are not scheduled. I often see students when I am working in the library. One day, three of us converged in the same aisle looking for the same journal and article. We had all used the Infotrac computer for our search and had very similar printouts of possible sources. The journal we were all looking for was missing from the shelves.

In response to their complaints of not being able to find any of the material in the library, I ran through the drill: Did you check with the reference librarian? Did you check the reshelving carts? Did you walk around to see if anyone was using it? Did you check to see if it was on microfilm? After this discussion, we divided the remaining list of sources and went searching again. We met half an hour later and between us we had all of the articles we wanted. At the very least, when I see students in the library, we compare notes and offer each other help. I notice a difference in students' attitude and participation in class after I have met them in the library. They are more open, interested, and committed to the collaborative process.

Thorough Involvement

During class, I visit every group, engage in small group discussions, listen to students talk about their process, and offer suggestions to help facilitate their work. I also share resources and offer other perspectives they might want to consider. The level of interaction with those groups working on the same topic as I is somewhat more intense. Students seem more willing to include me in their discussions because we are both dealing with the same material. Our discussions are more substantial. Because of this higher level of academic discourse, I choose my topics to investigate according to which students I need to work with in this way. By working with students in the library and in class, I believe I both instruct in and model the behaviors of critical scholarship.

Testing

The questions that direct our work set the foundation for class discussions and become questions on essay tests. The students and I sit in a large circle and listen critically to each other's presentations. We take our own notes and challenge points that seem unreasonable. It is not uncommon, for example, for anyone to challenge the findings of a research study based on the date or design of the study. It is also not uncommon for us to challenge each other's point of view using data to support our position. In fact, students challenge much more freely than I do. Bringing whole-class discussions to a conclusion involves agreeing on which information we accept as course content and are thereby responsible for knowing.

THE KEY: HEALTHY GROUP DYNAMICS

Theory and practical models aside, putting students together to work on a common assignment does not guarantee that Cooperative Learning will occur. Cooperative Learning is based on interdependence—the ability to work well together, using each other's strengths and weaknesses in a complementary manner in order to accomplish the task.

The success of a group's work is contingent, therefore, on a healthy interaction between students. Johnson and his colleagues (Johnson, 1990; Johnson & Johnson, 1991, Johnson, Johnson, & Smith, 1991a, 1991b) provide group dynamic formats that set the tone for productive, authentic work.

A healthy interaction begins with an awareness of the social skills needed for successful cooperative work: leadership, shared decision making, trust, effective communication, and conflict management. These skills are developed through the use of warm-up exercises, social tasks, group roles, and the processing of group work once the assignment is complete (Johnson, Johnson, & Smith, 1991a, 1991b).

Warm-up exercises are directed toward the whole class during the first week of the semester. I explain to students that the course structure of group work requires us to know each other enough to work well together and warm-ups help "break the ice." Depending on the exercise, we will spend 5 to 20 minutes at the beginning of the first two, maybe three, classes of the semester. These activities help build community both inside and outside the classroom.

The assignment of a social task at the beginning of each group session further breaks down the barriers between students. Social tasks range from introducing each other by name, the meaning of their names, or a memory cue that helps others remember their names to a sharing of their academic strengths, academic weaknesses, or style of conflict management.

By learning more about each other, students find a common ground that gives them something to identify with and connect with in each other. This familiarity through self-disclosure transcends the stereotypical first impression that students have of each other and helps them to begin to recognize each other's limitations and potential. I find that this knowledge leads to an appreciation and acceptance of the other. This familiarity also induces students to accept more responsibility for their contributions to the group.

The assignment of a social task at the beginning of each group session further breaks down the barriers between students. Social tasks range from introducing each other by name, the meaning of their names, or a memory cue that helps others remember their names to a sharing of their academic strengths, academic weaknesses, or style of conflict management. By learning more about each other, students find a common ground that gives them something to identify with and connect with in each other.

Assigning Roles

Appropriate social skills are further developed through the use of group roles during the small-group session. Besides the academic task, each student takes on added responsibilities. Johnson, Johnson, and Smith (1991a, 1991b) suggest a number of group roles that create social interdependence among students. Figure 2.1 contains the roles used in my classes.

The use of group roles encourages equal participation of group members where everyone has the opportunity to participate without one person dominating. Equal participation may not occur, but the structure is there, and, as a result, students recognize that everyone has valuable contributions to make to the group, which, in turn, helps it run efficiently and effectively. Students choose roles among themselves but are encouraged to take a turn at each role throughout the semester. When I check in with each group, I ask who is functioning in which role. Frequently, I will also ask which roles each student has taken on so far in the semester and make a note of those students who need to move on to other roles. The next time group roles are chosen, I will remind those students of what roles they need to try.

Figure 2.1
Group Roles

RECORDER	Takes notes during the group discussion and compiles a presentation for the whole class.
REPORTER	Presents the group information to the class.
CHECKER	Monitors the group members' understanding of the topic under discussion and stops the group work for clarification when someone is confused.
ENCOURAGER	Ensures that everyone has the opportunity to participate in the group's work and praises members for their contributions.
OBSERVER	Monitors and records the overall behaviors of the group according to an agreed upon checklist of behaviors.

Developing appropriate social skills continues even after the group work is finished through the processing of group work for evaluation purposes. The same format is used for small groups and whole-class discussions. Following Johnson, Johnson, and Smith's (1991a, 1991b) model, students are asked to list three things they found helpful and one thing they would like to see improved. Students are encouraged to look at the behaviors of others, not personalities, in an effort to identify those specific behaviors that facilitate group work and those that hinder it. This information is then shared with either the small group or the whole class.

Students are encouraged to be constructive and communicate with each other appropriately by using language that is nonthreatening and nondefensive. In other words, students are instructed to describe a behavior rather than judge it, to remove the words *you should* from their vocabulary and replace them with *could you* or *you might*, and to take responsibility for their thoughts and feelings by using the word *I* instead of *we, you,* or *they.*

It's Almost Perfect

Student feedback from both introductory and developmental psychology courses has been extremely positive. I obtain direct feedback on the course structure by asking students to evaluate the small-group work. I receive indirect feedback by periodically asking students to anonymously respond in writing to the question: "What is the most significant learning that has occurred as a result of this course?"

In both cases, students report that they learn more information and learn it better, that their own perspective broadens because they have the opportunity of hearing others' points of view, which forced them to rethink their own, that they learn how to work with others, and that they learn to respect others. Students in the Collaborative Learning groups additionally report that they learn how to use libraries, do research, interpret primary sources, and question nonprimary sources.

Race Relations Improve

Johnson, Johnson, and Smith (1991a, 1991b), Kagan (cited in Brandt, 1989/90), and Slavin (1989/1990) have found that group work also improves self-esteem, interpersonal relationships, and race relations. I agree.

Cooperative and collaborative learning provide a format for dealing with diversity, both in terms of a multicultural curriculum and student skill levels. As students begin to feel safe in a classroom environment that is respectful, their questioning process becomes more open and honest.

Confronted for the first time perhaps with lifestyles unlike their own and influenced by the media's coverage of society, students express interest in African-American, Hispanic, gay/lesbian concerns, and others. In Cooperative Learning classes, I respond to these interests by helping students access the information they are looking for. Students in Collaborative Learning classes respond to these interests by introducing studies on their particular concern or concerns into the course content via their small-group investigations and presentations during whole-class discussions.

Studying course content, hearing other students' perspectives, and getting to know students of diverse backgrounds while working with them influences attitudinal changes. Students also recognize in themselves and others their strengths and weaknesses and how these complement the working of a group. Students then report a change in attitude toward themselves, people of varying skill levels, people of color, gays and lesbians, and people of all ages.

Tolerance Increases

Influenced by these attitudinal changes, students have also reported a change in their behaviors. They report being more accepting and respectful. These behaviors are noticeable in the classroom and in student conversations. These changes will help students live more productive, useful, and healthy lives in the workplace, but also in their families, neighborhoods, and communities.

Grades Improve

Student success can be measured from student reports, both solicited and unsolicited, plus their grades. Students in cooperative and collaborative learning courses have a higher rate of above-average grades. The percent of students in my courses receiving a grade of "B" or better has risen from an average of 60 percent to 85 percent for those students who complete the course. This scholastic success seems to be due to the ownership students share in the course content.

The material is covered in a way that is meaningful and useful to students, and their work is authentic. These grades do not reflect simple grade inflation. A comparison of my syllabi indicates that students are doing more work, being challenged more intellectually than students in my earlier classes, yet earning higher grades. In addition, students report that the skills they learn in my courses help them to be more successful in their other courses regardless of that course's structure.

A LOT OF HARD WORK

As rewarding and successful as group work is, facilitating group work can be very difficult. It is tedious work to visit each group, explaining and re-explaining the tasks at hand, reminding students of their roles, modeling those roles when necessary, and prodding everyone along. It is also time- and energy-consuming to be involved in reflective teaching, with its constant need for observation, interaction, and analysis of student progress, the classroom environment, and my own behaviors. Yet this is a crucial element in both the cooperative and collaborative learning structures because what works with one class or one student may not work with everyone.

Often the energy consumed by reflective teaching and the flexibility required to produce a successful learning situation precludes implementing, in each course every semester, all of the social skill processes. During a recent semester, for example, one class did not evaluate small-group work at all or follow through consistently in group roles. I was not concerned, however, as these students, having been exposed to the process of group work, were closer to developing the necessary cooperative skills than they were before.

TACKLING THE UNKNOWN

The most frustrating aspect of cooperative or collaborative work, however, is moving students from the familiar product-oriented education to the unfamiliar process approach to education. Students involved in collaborative learning groups have a difficult time at first accepting the notion of providing their own information for the course, providing the "meat" of the course, as they have called it.

Some students also have difficulty accepting the effectiveness, on a continuous basis, of the three social skills processes: social tasks, group roles, and the processing of group work. These students believe that knowing about group process and experiencing it once is enough. They do not realize that they could be more productive if they improved their group effectiveness and that improving group effectiveness takes time and practice in developing the appropriate relationships and social skills.

RE-ENVISIONING CONTENT

Finally, facilitating group work is difficult because it takes time away from course content, although learning the process is part of the content. Given the short amount of time and the amount of material that is expected to be covered in any given semester, however, I am always faced with the tension of balancing group work with content. I have come though to two conclusions: less really is more and the time involved in developing appropriate relationships and social skills is time well-spent.

Students may cover less topical material but cover it more in-depth. They are, in fact, covering far more material than would normally be anticipated, and they are able to make connections between topics. I have noticed, for example, that class discussions in my courses have moved from static, segregated topical discussions to broad-ranging, all-encompassing discussions that flow more smoothly and represent the students' ability to make connections and synthesize ideas. When students develop the appropriate working relationships, they work more efficiently and are more productive.

TRY IT, YOU MIGHT LIKE IT!

My use of cooperative and collaborative learning may not be appropriate for everyone, but it at least provides an experiential model for some. Because professors are so involved in the learning process of their students when engaged in cooperative or collaborative learning, it is critical for them to follow a design that is comfortable and works for them. The best way to know what works for you is to experiment with cooperative or collaborative learning techniques in your own classes. Read the literature, gather your own data, and know that your students benefit from the process even if it is not perfect.

Integrating these strategies into your courses may be easier if they are introduced slowly, one course or one strategy at a time. I would suggest any of David W. Johnson's books as helpful resources for those professors concerned with specific strategies. My courage to develop course strategies inconsistent with the traditional approach to education, however, came from Freire (1970). Those engaged in this type of exploration will discover, as I did, that their techniques evolve with ongoing investigations and professional development.

Regardless of the techniques I employ, my use of group work will continue to be fueled by the desire to have students learn well and develop the mutual respect that is critical within our society.

NOTES

1. Slavin argues that student achievement improves through cooperative learning only when two conditions are present: group goals are shared and individual accountability is in place. He does, however, point out that while research supports the influence of these conditions in elementary and secondary schools, the work of Davidson (1985 cited in Slavin, 1989/90) and Dansereau (1988, cited in Slavin 1989/90) indicates that they may not be necessary at the college level.

2. Student self-reports and observations continue to generate data. Self-reports of a structured interview format consist of the processing of group work after a completed task, periodic and brief course evaluations throughout the semester, and a more detailed course evaluation at the end of the semester. I record naturalistic observations of the behaviors of interest during or after class as the situation presents itself.

REFERENCES

Aronson, E., Blaney, N., Stephan, C., Sikes, J., & Snapp, M. (1978). *The Jigsaw Classroom*. Beverly Hills, CA: Sage Publications, Inc.

Belenky, M. F., Clinchy, B. M., Goldberger, N. R., & Tarule, J. M. (1986). *Women's Ways of Knowing: The Development of Self, Voice, and Mind*. New York: Basic Books.

Brandt, R. (1989/90). On cooperative learning: A conversation with Spencer Kagan. *Educational Leadership* 47(4): 8-11.

Freire, P. (1970). *Pedagogy of the Oppressed*. New York: Herder and Herder.

Jackson, S. C. (1986). Consultation and collaboration through cooperative goal structures: A pilot study. *College Student Journal* 20(1): 47-50.

Johnson, D. W. (1993). *Reaching Out: Interpersonal Effectiveness and Self-Actualization*. 5th ed. Needham Heights, MA: Allyn and Bacon.

Johnson, D. W., & Johnson, R. T. (1991). *Joining Together: Group Theory and Group Skills*. Boston: Allyn and Bacon.

Johnson, D. W., Johnson, R. T., & Smith, K. A. (1991a). *Active Learning: Cooperation in the College Classroom*. Edina, MN: Interaction Book Co.

————. (1991b). *Cooperative Learning: Increasing College Faculty Instructional Productivity*. Washington, DC.: The George Washington University.

Johnson, R. E. (1975). Meaning in complex learning. *Review of Educational Research* 45(3): 425-59.

Kagan, S. (1989/90). The structural approach to cooperative learning. *Educational Leadership* 47(4): 12-15.

McDougall. K., & Gimple, D. (1985). *"Cooperative Learning Strategies for Teaching Small Group Communication: Research and Application."* Paper presented at the 71st Annual Meeting of the Speech Communication Association, Denver, CO. November 7-10.

Schultz, D. P., & Schultz, S. E. (1990). *Psychology and Industry Today.* 5th ed. New York: Macmillan Publishing Co.

Sizer, T. R. (1984). *Horace's Compromise: The Dilemma of the American High School.* Boston: Houghton Mifflin Co.

————. (1992). *Horace's School: Redesigning the American High School.* Boston: Houghton Mifflin Co.

Slavin, R. E. (1989/90). Research on cooperative learning: Consensus and controversy. *Educational Leadership* 47(4): 52-54.

Tompkins, J. (1990). Pedagogy of the distressed. *College English* 52(6): 653-60.

3

THE INDIVIDUAL AND THE GROUP AS TECHNOLOGY-BASED PROBLEM SOLVERS

by Bill Yates

For much of history, petroglyphs, hieroglyphics, and other forms of writing were our only means of recording thoughts and ideas. Then the Gutenberg printing press spawned a revolution in the way people dealt with their world. What a revolutionary effect the device had on the generations to come. It is probably no coincidence that within a century after the invention of the printing press, the scientific revolution had begun and books had become commonplace. Now it seems that the computer will exert as great an influence as the printing press, having already established itself as a device that not only stores information but also enhances human reasoning power (Searles, 1983).

The amount of information that humans have accumulated is so overwhelming that any one person or group of people can retain and use only a small percentage of it. The American Library Directory lists the number of books, pamphlets, and other holdings in the Library of Congress at eighty million and that does not include the literature in other regions of the world. Knowledge in some disciplines is so voluminous that to specialize and become an expert necessitates defining a narrow area of the domain.

To make the situation even more complex, the basic technology needed to handle the information load changes monthly. A few years ago personal computers had memories in the kilobytes and now it is common to find them with many megabytes of memory. This increase in memory size and the corresponding increase in processing speed has added another dimension to the software used to manage the data. Furthermore, CD-ROM technology is becoming commonplace and that technology is also changing rapidly.

At times it is overwhelming to the college classroom professor. It is virtually impossible to keep up with information and with the changing technologies used to manage that information. Given the fact that the educational needs of our students fill our day, we have little time to deepen our understanding of these changes around us.

To cope with these changes requires a new perspective, a more effective way of doing things, in short a change in paradigm. That is why many educational leaders have emphasized the shift from an industrial model of education that depended upon a population that knew basic language and math skills with emphasis on content and rote recall to a generalized information age model that better meets the needs of our students.

The information age model of education changes both the role of the professor and the nature of the curriculum. For example, professors cannot expect to master even a small percentage of the overall knowledge of a subject. This means that we can no longer place a high value on the intrinsic knowledge level of teachers; instead we must encourage teachers to develop their ability to moderate and interpret vast amounts of information. The teacher must become more a guide and less a giver of facts. This is not to say that facts are not important. It merely represents a change in emphasis. The teacher becomes a person who is able to gather information, relate facts, explain inferences, form generalizations, and transfer these same abilities to students (Rooze, 1986). The information age model requires teaching skills that address the needs of today's world, such as inquiry, critical thinking, decision making, and information processing abilities (Yates & Moursund, 1988). Students need to be taught to be lifelong learners, because content knowledge in all disciplines will continue to increase at a rapid rate and no one person can assimilate all of the available knowledge. Andrew R. Molnar (1979-80) of the National Science Foundation has said, "If we are to master information, we must expand human ability to learn and comprehend, and we must create new intellectual tools to extend human capacity to reason and to work smarter" (p. 33).

Even industrial and economic leaders are recognizing

the need for positive change in our educational methodologies because of world economic conditions. For example, Robert M. Solow (1988), the Nobel Prize winning economist, indicates that the major driving force behind our economic growth is technology. Not only are capital and labor important, but so is technology. To use that technology we need an educated citizenry. If we intend to continue our economic growth, we need to invest heavily in training and education that emphasizes information age skills.

Within the setting of rapid changes in the world and the pressure on our educational systems to change, there are three generalizations that capture the essence of the educational process. Students retain their individuality and are inherent problem solvers. All students work cooperatively within groups to solve problems. And all students, in order to compete, use technology to assist in their problem-solving efforts.

We need to have a deeper understanding of the individual problem solver and the group processes that facilitate problem solving. The rest of this chapter examines first, some of what is known about human problem solvers, second, principles of Cooperative Learning and collaboration that aid in solving problems in a group setting, and third, how technology can be used to assist the individual and the group to become better problem solvers.

THE INDIVIDUAL AND PROBLEM SOLVING

Problem solving is a learned skill and a basic skill. How individuals develop this skill is not fully understood. However, researchers are beginning to identify some of the processes that enhance problem-solving ability. The following are a few ideas from the research that if coupled with good Cooperative Learning and collaborative strategies make for a stronger problem-solving environment.

Precise thinking (or processing) is one of the keys to strong problem-solving ability. Whimbey (1984), in reviewing the research of Bloom and others, concludes that the difference between good problem-solving styles and poor problem-solving styles is in the depth of processing. The students with good problem-solving skills tend to employ a lengthy sequential analysis in arriving at an answer; whereas, the the students with poor problem-solving styles tend to take a very superficial or one-shot thinking approach to a problem. Precise processing is the key attribute of higher-order thinking. This means more emphasis should be placed on mental processing, with provisions made to observe and guide individuals with feedback on their processing.

How conscious we are of our thinking processes while solving a problem is dependent on whether we are using a familiar strategy or having to develop the strategy as we work (Kellogg, 1982). Some psychologists have argued that when we introspect and verbalize how we are solving a problem, we give an accurate portrayal of how we are solving a problem; others have suggested that much of what is involved is unconscious, and therefore, verbalizations are not an accurate description of a problem-solving process. Kellogg gives evidence that both views may be true, depending on the type of task involved. If the problem requires conscious effort, then verbalizing may provide an accurate picture, but if the task uses automatic procedures (previously learned problem-solving methods), then the procedures may not be reflected in the verbal reports. We have all prepared a meal that required very little thought for each procedure. Once we proceduralize a process, we can do it without thinking explicitly about the steps.

If a person thinks deeply about a problem, any spurious event may trigger a solution—even an event not consciously perceived (Yaniv & Meyer, 1987). Yaniv and Meyer attempted to measure the activation and metacognition of inaccessible information by testing the memory-sensitization hypothesis. This hypothesis says that a failed attempt to solve a problem may partially activate stored but inaccessible information that is critical to the solution. During an intervening period some event may trigger the information critical to the solution. Yaniv and Meyer's study supports the hypothesis.

The unconscious mind may be the repository of many of our procedural steps for solving problems. The associations made between procedural elements and facts at this level is unknown. How we sort and search through these options is unknown. But the sensitization of memory may prime mental processes that can more easily retrieve the information.

An extraordinary memory may not enhance problem-solving skills. Rather, a carefully refined set of problem-solving strategies may more significantly influence performance in a given domain (Simon & Simon, 1962). The Simon and Simon study looks at how world-class chess players go about playing championship chess. They suggest that the large memory and processing capabilities of outstanding chess players is a myth. To examine all the possible moves of a complex chess position requires over a billion combinatorial views. To examine all these combinations would be a prodigious mental feat, but it seems that grand-master chess players do not review all the possible moves. They use a powerful selective general strategy learned from experience. Thus, grand masters do not need large memories or very fast processing capacities, because through long practice they develop a very selective but effective problem-solving strategy.

Thus, facts and information alone are not enough to solve a problem. An efficient process for organizing and managing that information is also an important element in problem solving. A limited number of effective procedures is more important than a large amount of information that cannot be accessed or ordered in a way that leads to a solution.

Metacognition

Thinking about the problem is an important problem-solving strategy long known by educators. Verbalizing the problem as we solve it also seems to help. Problem solvers who talk about the steps they are taking do better than those who do not describe their efforts (Gagne & Smith, 1962; Berry, 1983; Bender, 1986). Gagne (1962) conducted a study to determine the effects of verbalization on problem-solving ability. The subjects were freshman and sophomore high school students. The students who talked with others about how they were attempting to solve the problem, solved problems better than those who did not verbalize their thinking processes.

Those who were required to verbalize their solutions also solved the problems in a shorter period of time. Gagne suggests that verbalization has the effect of making the students examine alternative lines of reasoning, thus facilitating the discovery of general rules and the application of these rules to other like problems.

Berry (1983) studied the process of transfer of problem-solving skills from concrete to more abstract problems. While solving problems, the subjects who were allowed to talk to others about how they were thinking through their solution did better on more abstract tasks than those who were not allowed to talk as they were solving similar problems. Having to consciously verbalize what one is doing is an explicit form of metacognition. Thinking about how we think seems to reinforce our thought processes. It is theorized that verbalization may lead to an increased awareness of past behavior, specifically those aspects of awareness that are necessary for a successful resolution of the problem.

Framing Goals

Even with well-structured problems like math problems, people tend to frame small subgoals and may not be able to explain why they did so (Greeno, 1976). Greeno has found that when people solve a well-defined problem such as proving a theorem in high school geometry, they develop numerous small subgoals that are not always well-defined (indefinite goals). When encountering a problem, an individual typically sets many subgoals without knowing how the information obtained will be used. This same phenomenon has been observed in problem situations. This process of trying different options may be an attempt to find a line of reasoning that will allow for a partial or complete solution. Apparently framing small subgoals is an unconscious act as the human mind struggles with the new problem's structure.

Changing our perspective on a problem often aids in arriving at a solution (Scheerer, 1983). Scheerer has found that when solving a problem you can and should change your approach. Several experiments have shown that when problem solvers become "fixated" with one approach to the problem, the solution process is inhibited. Subjects who changed their perspective and tried a different approach arrived at an answer quicker than those who persisted in only one approach. Often sudden shifts in perspective facilitate problem solving.

Any problem has a limited number of solution paths. When choosing a path that does not lead to a solution, we fail. By changing our perspective we can find a path that does lead to a solution. A person's natural tendency is to attain a state of mental equilibrium. This need provides the impetus to change our perspective but this change does not come without effort.

Individual Personality

There is a strong correlation between self-image and how well you can solve a problem. Individuals who perceive themselves to be strong problem solvers take more time to encode information and think about it before acting on it and in so doing seem to be more efficient at problem solving (Armstrong & McDaniel, 1986). Self-image is a strong determiner of how most of us act in any given situation. The self-knowledge of our expertise may provide the cognitive environment conducive to efficient processing of information. Anecdotal reports by some artists suggest that a deep sense of confidence often supports their artistic problem-solving efforts.

Some studies (Ross, 1983; Mayer, 1983) support the notion that if elements of a personal nature are included in a problem, the problem becomes more meaningful and motivation to solve the problem seems to increase. In situations where the problem has a meaningful context, more personal ownership is attached to the problem, which provides a motivational force that improves performance by the students. The ownership necessary for a person to become involved in problem solving has been discussed in the works of Moursund (1986) and others. If a person is indifferent to a problem, he or she has no inclination to solve it. Most people have an intuitive feeling for what is meant by ownership in problem solving. This feeling is the emotive bridge between inaction and action. Ownership is the conceptual structure that is built between an individual need to solve the problem and the procedural and informational schema necessary to solve the problem.

Transfer of Skills

Another critical element in problem solving is the ability to apply the learned skill in other settings. One way to facilitate transfer of skills to other problem-solving domains is through guided discovery. The ownership acquired in such an environment may be a strong contributor to the elements that allow transfer to occur. When a person arrives at a solution through guided discovery in one setting, there is some indication that the skills learned in that setting can be more easily applied to other settings (Mayer & Greeno, 1975; Reed, Ernst, & Banerji, 1974; Royer, 1979). Mayer's research on transfer of learning suggests that *near-transfer* (transfer of skills to problems similar to those already solved by the individual) and *far-transfer* (transfer to a different or novel setting) can be enhanced. Mayer looked at the differences between learning outcomes produced by different methods of instruction. With university students as experimental subjects, Mayer used direct instruction to teach one group about the binomial distribution concept and used the same material but with a discovery-based approach to teach the other group. Mayer found that students in the discovery-based learning group had stronger far-transfer than those in the direct instruction group. Having to integrate information in our conceptual matrix or consciously process a series of steps in a procedure allow our cognitive frameworks to act on the information and personalize it. This may establish an association between the residential mental structures and the new material. Integrating the new ideas rather than passively accepting the information probably results in the individual attaching more meaning to the material. This integration may allow far-transfer to occur, because the person understands within the context of the experience the applicability of the material and has formed the associative pathways to relate the experience to other situations.

Reed, Ernst, and Banerji (1974) studied how solving one problem helped in solving another problem of a similar type. They concluded that without help from another person there is no substantive transfer of skills. However, there is a transfer of skills when a subject solves the same problem again. They found that when another person suggested that the problems had similar characteristics, there was some transfer, but the transfer was not dramatic enough to be conclusive.

It takes many years to become an expert. To develop the conceptual reflexes to take a broad knowledge base and link with a large number of effective procedures takes a long time. Concentrated attention and long practice is necessary it seems before expertise can be expressed easily and a solution just seems to "come to us." However, experts working outside of their area of expertise do no better than novices (Simon & Simon, 1962). Expert chess players do no better than the average person when encountering unique problems. The same seems to be true for experts in general. The expert has to go through the same mental steps all people use when encountering a new problem or problem situation. If the problem is similar to one experienced in the expert's area of expertise, then the transfer of skills may allow the expert to learn faster. However, most people approach new experiences the same way. At first they work hard to arrive at a solution, and then later learn to do it effortlessly. Thus with experience we improve as problem solvers, but we seem to have difficulty transferring that knowledge to analogous problems in other domains.

Thinking about Problems

How we think about a problem and how we represent the problem are indicator of how well we will solve it. The research suggests that we should take time to try and find the best representation of the problem before attempting a solution.

How we think about (or represent) a problem is a better indicator of the problem's difficulty than any quality intrinsic to the logic of the problem (Frederiksen, 1984; Kotovsky, Hayes, & Simon, 1985). Frederiksen (1984) summarizes the research on the relationship between problem representation and ease of solution. Lacking a complete representation of the interrelationship between the elements of a problem will influence the quality of the problem's solution.

It is interesting to note that when asked to categorize problems on the basis of similarities in methods of solution, novices tended to sort problems by superficial features primarily comprised of facts. Experts, tended to represent the problem in terms of schema containing both factual and procedural knowledge of solution methods. It seems that good problem solvers have a better mental representation of the problem.

According to Kotovsky (1985), a good external representation is helpful in problem solving. Using the Tower of Hanoi problem, Kotovsky et al. found that the memory load is reduced by external memory aids and thus presumably provides more resources for higher-order processing. This is consistent with the view that short-term memory resources and higher-order mental processes are limited. Therefore, allocation of these resources becomes an important consideration when solving new or difficult problems requiring a lot of conscious effort.

Types of Problems

The type of problem determines what type of solution occurs to the individual. A problem that can be solved sequentially or incrementally does not require a significant amount of insight or creative effort to find new steps. Problems with less structure may require more insight to solve (Metcalfe & Wiebe, 1987).

A visual representation of a problem can facilitate analogical reasoning by acting as a retrieval cue (Beveridge & Parkins, 1987). The visual component of our experience may be the most important of all our sensory inputs. We see patterns and integrate and respond to those patterns. Many patterns can be represented graphically in math, science, and the social studies. By such representations, ideas can be concretized. The concretized ideas can then be retrieved by such visual cues. This supports the intuition of many good problem solvers and suggests that representing the ideas and subgoals pictorially can help in solving a problem. Perhaps from these visual cues new patterns can be developed that lead to a solution to the problem.

Limitations of Problem Solving

There are limitations to problem solving across disciplines. In a review of essays from psychologists, mathematicians, and computer scientists dealing with heuristics and other problem-solving skills, Groner (1983) concludes that no general themes can be found among problem solvers that can be applied across disciplines. The diverse quality of intellectual and social activities suggests that the resultant complexity of many problems reflect that diversity and thus cannot be reduced to a few algorithms or heuristic steps.

But a number of general problem-solving heuristics advocated by researchers and educators, while not applicable across all disciplines, do seem to capture some qualities that make them useful in an educational setting. For example, many years ago Wallas (1926) advocated four steps for solving a problem: Preparation, Incubation, Illumination, and Verification. More recently, Polya (1968) suggested these problem-solving steps: understand the problem, devise a plan, carry out the plan, and look back to analyze the solution.

For primary and secondary education, Moursund (1986) synthesizes much of the literature and suggests a problem-solving approach that combines certain aspects of Dewey's philosophy and Polya's (1968) model of problem solving. He defines formal problems as having four qualities: givens, guidelines, goals, and ownership. The givens are what is known about the problem at the beginning. Guidelines are the steps or rules that can be used to work toward the end or goal. The goal is the desired end result or final solution. Ownership or investment in the problem requires that the person solving a problem have some personal investment in its solution. Ownership, according to Moursund, plays a central role in problem solving.

Thus, understanding the problem is the most important initial step. This may involve determining what is known about the problem, analyzing the end or goal, and determining the necessary operations.

Moursund also suggests several rules of thumb that can be used to help solve a problem. The first rule of thumb, is to make an effort to understand the problem. This requires domain-specific knowledge, but it is helpful to have a broad experiential background. The second rule of thumb is to build upon the work of others. This eliminates the need to rethink or redo what has already been done by someone else. The third rule of thumb is to improve problem-solving abilities by *practicing* problem-solving methods. The third rule has the strongest support in the literature on problem solving (Frederiksen, 1984).

According to Moursund (1986), problem situations, that are problem-like but missing one or more of the formal components should be recast into a formal problem structure whenever possible. Viewing the problem situation in a more formal problem structure forces the problem solver into more familiar modes of investigation and possibly helps to resolve the situation.

What makes this approach to problem solving attractive is its congruence with much of what is known about human problem solvers. In addition, it offers a process that can be applied to less formally defined subjects like history and social studies. This schema provides a clearly delineated process coupled with heuristics that have some experimental support. It also provides a conceptual bridge between informal problem situations and formal problem structures.

As can be seen from the brief review of the research, some things are known about how people do problem solving, but human problem solving is a very complex and little understood set of processes. No clear, proven theories have emerged.

The ultimate purpose behind the research is to gain a deeper understanding of human problem-solving processes so that educators can focus their efforts on problem-solving skills that are prerequisites for later learning. In this way optimal use can be made of the limited learning time available to the student in today's formal educational system.

COOPERATIVE LEARNING AND CONSULTATION

A technologically based society is dependent on individuals who can think for themselves and with others. It requires individuals who can communicate effectively with all types of people and with highly varied groups. Such skills need to be taught explicitly in the classroom, especially through the methodology of Cooperative Learning. Johnson and Johnson's (1989) research on Cooperative Learning strongly supports the notion that more effective problem solving occurs when problems are encountered and handled by a group rather than by individuals. The ability to work well with other individuals in a problem-solving environment is critical. Thus, the underlying structure of communication must be based on mutual respect and courtesy for other persons' viewpoints. These communication skills need to be explicitly identified and taught to the students (Foyle, Lyman, & Alexander-Thies, 1991).

Successful collaboration requires a clear understanding of the problem and the facts associated with the problem, an open and courteous attitude toward ideas as they are shared and explored by the group, an agreed-upon set of general rules or principles that apply to the problem's solution, and an applicable and agreed-on strategy to solve the problem (Kolstoe, 1985).

Kolstoe says that consultation "is both a means of jointly considering something and a means of allowing an idea to grow. There is a unique blend of experience, knowledge, minds, hearts, feelings, hopes and fears. In a condition of suspended judgment these combine to allow the development of an idea, a transformation which comes about when there is a sincere exchange. Generally the final result is quite different from either the original thought or any of the specific additional contributions. It is neither a compromise nor the simple addition of one thought to another: it is a new creation" (pp. 8-9).

As educators, we must model a safe consultative environment for our students. Without a disciplined effort on our part to direct the collaborative energies along a productive path and thus instill in our students healthy ways of group discourse, we cannot hope to enhance group problem-solving skills (Yates & Foyle, 1992).

There is some research that supports the idea of using technology to enhance the problem-solving environment. Scott (1993) found that using technology increased productivity and enhanced participation within the social group using computer-mediated communications. In a collection of articles edited by Mavarech and Light (1992), contributors indicate that computers facilitate learning in a cooperative setting. Evidence continues to mount that computers properly used in a cooperative setting enhance group problem-solving efficiency, self-concept, and attitudes in the educational environment (Apple Computer, 1991).

COMPUTER TECHNOLOGY AND EDUCATION

The computer brings a particularly useful set of characteristics to the collaborative and group problem-solving environment. In the classroom, the professor is busy managing the class and the resources that maximize the learning opportunities. By using the computer to manage many of the details associated with sequencing the resources in "real time," the teacher is free to focus more time and energy on teaching thinking and consultative skills (Yates & Foyle, 1992). This is but one example of how technology can help our teachers teach problem-solving skills to our students.

Simulations

Many educators believe that the computer is a strong tool for helping solve problems as well as for helping to teach problem-solving skills (Kendall & Budin, 1987; Moursund, 1987; Schug & Kepner, 1984). Some curricular programs have been built around the computer, and the results, while not dramatic, indicate that the use of the computer is a plus not only for developing higher-order thinking skills but also as a tool to help teach basic skills (Pogrow, 1985). Computer simulations provide good problem-solving experiences because they provide a greater level of sophistication than similar simulations used without computers (Schug, 1984).

There are many ways that technology can help both the professor and the student. The computer can be used to model or simulate real-life situations, which brings added power to the instructional process. A variety of simulations are available to the educator. Broderbund (Murphey & Turner, 1989) produces *Where in the World Is Carmen Sandiego?* and MECC (1988) produces *The Oregon Trail*—two very successful simulations that have been widely used by educators in the classroom. Many others are available and can be useful additions to the learning environment.

Just as the computer can teach basic skills as well or better than traditional methods (Chambers, 1983), it can also assist in teaching certain problem-solving skills. For example, it has been shown that computerized science simulations can provide students with more productive practice in problem solving than other methods. Rivers and Vockell's (1987) study indicates that using a simulation improves the student's problem-solving and critical thinking abilities.

Databases

Educational research (Steinberg, Baskin, & Hofer, 1986) supports using databases in problem-solving activities. White (1987) notes that students can identify data to determine if the available data is enough to solve the problem and sort the data into new patterns to provide new insight into a problem. Students can collect their own data and develop their own databases. Students learn to disaggregate data, classify data, and use the scientific method as well as develop social skills needed to work with others (Yates & Moursund, 1988; Kendall & Budin, 1987).

The ability of databases to store, retrieve, and manipulate information gives the user tremendous power to manage information. Databases can search and sort data much more quickly than a person. But it is the person who needs the analytical skills to interpret the data. Thus, it becomes important to teach students inquiry, inference, and critical thinking skills. Many educators believe databases are useful in teaching such skills and are useful as professor-student tools in learning about problems and their resolutions (Yates, 1991; Hunter, 1985; Watson, 1989). Database software is common and easy to acquire. MacWorks® for the Mac environment and PC Works® for the MS-DOS environment are integrated word processing, spreadsheet, and database packages. These and many others are easily accessible database systems available to the educator.

On-line Systems

On-line systems have proliferated and are easily accessible through the Internet. This vast interconnected computerized network allows users to access an incredible number of databases that exist literally throughout the world. Indeed, pictures and text of the Dead Sea scrolls can be accessed by using the Internet to access libraries in the Middle East. Information exists in a wide variety of text, pictures, and database formats. There are also dozens of user groups on the Internet and these groups consult on a variety of subjects from current events to lesson plans for professors.

These databases along with a wide variety of commercially available databases containing data on virtually any subject, coupled with spreadsheets, word processing, simulations, graphing programs, other on-line resources, and generic computer applications fall into the general category of problem-solving tools. One only needs to access the Internet information superhighway to enter a mass of databases from around the world. While there are other ways to teach problem solving, the computer brings with it the ability to generate algorithmic solutions, apply problem-solving heuristics to limited domains of activity, provide more realistic simulations, search and sort data, and generate environments that allow for a greater degree of in-context practice on certain problem-solving skills both at the individual and group level.

Summary

In summary, as computer systems have become commonly available, educators have been forced to examine classroom applications of the computer, just as many math educators were forced to examine the role of the calculator in arithmetic (Moursund, 1981). The computer helps solve certain problems as well or better than people. Thus it may ultimately redirect educational forces away from outmoded skills and toward more useful skills that serve the needs of a more sophisticated and information-rich world.

Problem solving and Cooperative Learning are central to the information age model of education. The paradigm shift from the industrial to the information age has been brought about by cultural and economic factors both inside and outside of our society. The corresponding changes in our educational system have never been more important, and the need to respond to this shift has never been more critical to the intellectual and social development of our students. We need to teach basic skills in education. Two of the more important basic skills are problem solving and Cooperative Learning.

Technology is changing rapidly, so rapidly that a discussion of current technological systems now would be a dated discussion by the time this chapter goes to press. Problem solving, however, is here to stay. Even as technology changes, problem-solving strategies remain relatively constant. The "how-to" of technology, computers, and Cooperative Learning are readily available. However, the end result must be students who are strong problem solvers and capable of accepting and accommodating the changes in technology, in our society, and in an evolving world sociopolitical system.

REFERENCES

Apple Computer, Inc., (1991). *Apple Classroom of Tomorrow: Philosophy and Structure and What's Happening Where.* Cupertino, CA.

Armstrong, P., & McDaniel, E. (1986). Relationships between learning styles and performance on problem-solving tasks. *Psychological Reports* 59: 1135-1138.

Bender, T. A. (1986). Monitoring and the transfer of individual problem solving. *Contemporary Educational Psychology* 11: 161-69.

Berry, D. C. (1983). Metacognitive experience and transfer of logical reasoning. *The Quarterly Journal of Experimental Psychology* 35A: 39-49.

Beveridge, M., & Parkins, E. (1987). Visual representation in analogical problem solving. *Memory & Cognition* 15(3): 230-37.

Chambers, J. A. (1983). "Computer Assisted Instruction: Current Trends and Critical Issues." In D. O Harper & J. H. Stewart, *Run: Computer Education* (Dewey and Moursund 1986, 107-18). Monterey: Brooks/Cole Publishing Company.

Foyle, H. C., Lyman, L., & Alexander-Thies, S. (1991). *Cooperative Learning in the Early Childhood Classroom*. Washington, DC: National Education Association.

Frederiksen, N. (1984). Implications of cognitive theory for instruction in problem solving. *Review of Educational Research* 54(3): 363-407.

Gagne, R. M., & Smith, E. C. (1962). A study of the effects of verbalization on problem solving. *Journal of Experimental Psychology* 63(1): 12-18.

Greeno, J. G. (1976). Indefinite goals in well-structured problems. *Psychological Review* 83(6): 479-91.

Groner, R., Groner, M., & Bischof, W. F., eds. (1983). *Methods of Heuristics*. Hillsdale, NJ: Lawrence Eribaum Associates.

Hunter, B. (1985). Problem solving with databases. *The Computing Teacher* 12: 20-27.

Johnson, D. W., & Johnson, R. T. (1989). *Cooperation and Competition: Theory and Research*. Edina, MN: Interaction Book Company.

Kellogg, R. T. (1982). When can we introspect accurately about mental processes? *Memory and Cognition* 10(2): 141-44.

Kendall, D., & Budin, H. (1987). Computers for intellectual regeneration. (Interview with Robert Taylor). *Social Education* 51(1): 34-36.

Kolstoe, J. E. (1985). *Consultation: A Universal Lamp of Guidance*. Kidlington, Oxford: George Ronald Publishing.

Kotovsky, K., Hayes, J. R., & Simon, H. A. (1985). Why are some problems hard? Evidence from Tower of Hanoi. *Cognitive Psychology* 17: 248-94.

Mayer, R. E. (1983). *Thinking, Problem Solving, Cognition*. New York: W. H. Freeman and Company.

Mayer, R. E., & Greeno, J. G. (1975). Effects of meaningfulness and organization on problem solving and computability judgments. *Memory & Cognition* 3(4): 356-62.

Maverech, Z. R., & Light, P. H., eds. (1992). Cooperative learning and computers. *Learning and Instruction* 3(3): 55-285.

MECC. (1988). *The Oregon Trail.* (computer simulation). St. Paul, MN: Midwest Education Computer Consortium.

Metcalfe, J., & Wiebe, D. (1987). Intuition in insight and noninsight problem solving. *Memory and Cognition* 15(3): 238-46.

Molnar, A. R. (1979-80). Intelligent videodisc and the learning society. *The Journal of Educational Technology Systems* 8(1): 31-41.

Moursund, D. (1981). *Calculators in the Classroom.* New York: John Wiley & Sons.

———. (1986). *Computers and Problem Solving: A Workshop for Educators.* Eugene, OR: International Council for Computers in Education.

———. (1987). *Computers and Problem Solving: An Independent Study Course.* Eugene, OR: International Council for Computers in Education.

Murphey, C., & Turner, P. (1989). *Where in the World Is Carmen Sandiego.* (computer simulation). San Rafael, CA: Broderbund Software.

Pogrow, S. (1985). Helping students to become thinkers. *Electronic Learning* 4 (7): 26-29, 79.

Polya, G. (1968). "On Understanding Learning and Teaching Problem Solving." *Mathematical Discovery,* Vol. II. New York: Wiley.

Reed, S. K., Ernst, G. W., & Banerji, R. (1974). The role of analogy in transfer between similar problem states. *Cognitive Psychology* 6: 436-50.

Rivers, R. H., & Vockell, E. (1987). Computer simulations to stimulate scientific problem solving. *Journal of Research in Science Teaching* 24(5): 403-15.

Rooze, G. E. (1986). A strategy for helping students draw conclusions. The *Social Studies* 34: 74-76.

Ross, S. M. (1983). Increasing the meaningfulness of quantitative material by adapting context to student background. *Journal of Educational Psychology* 75: 519-29.

Royer, J. M. (1979). Theories of the transfer of learning. *Educational Psychologist* 14: 53-69.

Scheerer, M. (1983). Problem-solving. *Scientific American* 208(4): 118-28.

Schug, M. C., & Kepner, H. S., Jr. (1984). Choosing computer simulations in social studies. *The Social Studies* 75(5): 211-15.

Scott, D. M. (1993). "Teaching Collaborative Problem Solving Using Computer-Mediated Communications." Paper presented at the Annual

Meeting of the Association for Education and Communication Technology, New Orleans, LA, Jan. 13-17.

Searles, J. R. (1983). "Minds, Brains, and Programs." In D. R. Hofstadter and D. C. Dennett, eds. *The Mind's I.* New York: Basic Books.

Simon, H. A., & Simon P. A. (1962). Trial and error search in solving difficult problems: Evidence from the game of chess. *Behavioral Science* 7: 425-29.

Solow, R. M. (1988). *Growth Theory: An Exposition.* New York: Oxford University Press.

Steinberg, E. R., Baskin, A. B., & Hofer, E. (1986). Organizational/memory tools: A technique for improving problem solving skills. *Journal of Educational Computing Research* 2 (2): 169-87.

Wallas, G. (1926). *The Art of Thought.* New York: Harcourt Brace Jovanovich.

Watson, J. (1989). *Teaching Thinking Skills with Databases.* Eugene, OR: International Council for Computers in Education.

Whimbey, A. (1984). The key to higher-order thinking is precise processing. *Educational Leadership* 42(1): 66-70.

White, C. S. (1987). Developing information-processing skills through structured activities with a computerized file-management program. *Journal of Educational Computing Research* 3(3): 355-75.

Yaniv, I., & Meyer, D. E. (1987). Activation and metacognition of inaccessible stored information: Potential bases for incubation effects in problem solving. *Journal of Experimental Psychology: Learning, Memory, and Cognition* 13(2):187-205.

Yates, B. (1991). Databases in the science classroom. *Kansas Science Teacher* 8(1): 11-15.

Yates, B. C., & Foyle, H. C. (1992). Using the computer in the social studies classroom: Consultation and cooperative learning. *Computers in the Social Studies—A Journal for Educators* 1(1): 1-4.

Yates, B. C., & Moursund, D. (1988). The computer and problem solving: How theory can support classroom practice. *The Computing Teacher* 16(4): 12-16.

PART II

APPLICATIONS

Higher education faculty have a wide variety of collaborative, cooperative, and active learning approaches available for their use in the classroom. This section provides examples of several different approaches in various subject areas.

Scott Irwin provides specific lessons in science education that focus on group interactions and specific student roles within the groups. He centers his activity-based lessons on science experiments that provide experiences with the scientific method of investigation.

William G. Samuelson explains how to use a research approach called Group Investigation. He provides a step-by-step explanation of the use of Group Investigation in his Foundations of Education course. His explanation should allow any instructor to begin to implement this cooperative research method.

Jean Morrow in mathematics education provides insights into collaborative activities for face-to-face classes and for long distance learning. She believes that cooperative methods can help mathematics faculty implement the standards of the National Council of Teachers of Mathematics.

Connie S. Schrock indicates that cooperative groups are essential when students do original work or experiments. She provides examples of cooperative activities for various levels of mathematics courses. She points out that students must use and experience cooperative approaches during their own educational experiences so that they may have a better basis for their own careers.

Joanne M. Larson, in her reading classes, uses Think-Pair-Share, short projects, and semantic webbing in order to enhance student motivation. She uses collaborative strategies to help students learn to brainstorm and to deal with real issues that the students will face as classroom teachers.

In Peter Frederick's reprinted narration, he shares how to provide active learning in history courses. He suggests that instructors use numerous strategies such as interactive lectures, questions, small groups, problem solving and critical thinking, debates, role-playing, and audiovisual media. Each of these strategies involves the collaboration of students with students.

4

A COLLABORATIVE APPROACH TO ELEMENTARY SCIENCE METHODS

by Scott Irwin

It is only fair to begin this piece by admitting, for all the world to read, that the science methods course for preservice elementary teachers at Emporia State University (ESU) is probably *not so very unique*—at least in some respects. In fact, some of the course components most highly praised by students over the past two decades are simply examples of what effective teachers have been doing for a long time. There are, however, one or two dimensions of the science methods course at ESU that feature what we've come to call a "collaborative" approach to learning.

A LITTLE PERSPECTIVE

Like many such courses found in teacher education programs throughout the United States, EE 316, Teaching Science in the Elementary School (Irwin, 1994), is just one, 2-3 credit course in a 17-18 semester credit hour "package" of methods courses and classroom observation/teaching labs. Our preservice elementary teacher candidates complete this "Phase I" package as juniors or seniors, one or two semesters prior to student teaching. Furthermore, like most contemporary courses of its type, students in our science methods course work through a series of exercises to enhance their competence (and confidence) in the *problem-solving processes* of science and the *planning, teaching, and critiquing* of activity-based science experiences with children.

Just as in most such programs, EE 316 models what we hope to be exemplary science activities for preschool through middle school, with an ever-changing blend of "high-tech" and "grubby, no-tech" strategies and materials to serve students with diverse backgrounds and abilities. Many of the actual activities our science methods students complete have been lifted with little or no modification from the current array of process-oriented science curricula our students are likely to encounter among the materials in the University's Science/Mathematics Education Center and, later, as beginning teachers. Finally, just as it happens in most "mainstream" methods courses, the real "capstone" experience is the planning, teaching (with optional videotaping), and critiquing of one or more science lessons with children.

"So, what's *unique* about the elementary science methods course at Emporia State University?" you ask.

To begin with, students enter our "Phase I" package of methods courses, having already successfully completed a *minimum* of 11 semester hours in laboratory science courses, including a general biology course (3 hours); a second life science course (Robbins, 1994) designed exclusively for pre-service elementary teachers called Field and Lab Biology (GB 303, 3 hours); and an earth/physical science blend of laboratory activities (Keith & Thompson, 1994), also fine-tuned over two decades for elementary education majors, called Our Physical World (PS 115, 5 hours). The latter two courses are rigorous, laboratory-oriented science. They were developed by senior faculty in the College of Liberal Arts and Sciences through collaborative planning with professors in The Teachers College at Emporia State.

It is also important to note that these laboratory courses in the natural sciences and the methods courses in teacher education are all taught by tenure stream professors *who have public school science teaching experience.* These are *not* courses that get "dumped" on some graduate teaching assistant with little or no experience with K-8 students.

A CLOSER LOOK

The science methods course is set up on a competency-based model with a blended sequence of whole-class, small cooperative group, and individual activities. These activities lead to the achievement (or further enhancement) of a series of 23 competencies and two major outcomes in the problem-solving processes of science—ranging from simple observations using the senses to testing and revising hypotheses. The course also includes a second series of 14-15 competencies (leading to two more broad outcomes) in the planning, teaching, and critiquing of science experiences with children.

One or two days prior to beginning the course, a pair of diagnostic pretests is administered. These enable students and the instructor to determine those science process skills and teaching competencies already developed and those that need to be addressed.

The design, organization, and management of the course is such that when students are ready to begin "hands-on" activities in those problem-solving processes of science that they did *not* pretest out of, most work in small groups of two, three, or four—at their own pace. This part of science methods consumes at least *half* of the course's 32 class periods. During this time, the instructor does more indirect, responsive teaching, circulating among students, assisting them as *they* assume much of the responsibility/freedom in choosing: (a) the order in which a series of tasks are performed to achieve selected outcomes; (b) whether they pursue the tasks independently, as a member of a collaborative team of students, or in a tutorial mode with the instructor; (c) formal and/or informal methods of self-assessment of their progress; and (d) the extent to which they may want to use a given task as the basis for planning and teaching a science or interdisciplinary lesson with children.

Another interesting feature of using a comprehensive pretest to determine which science teaching exercises students do and do not need to complete is the fact that different students test out of different activities. This results in lots of opportunities to change partners from one activity to the next. For any given student, yesterday's lab partners might very well have quizzed out of (and, therefore not need to do) today's exercise. This creates opportunities for students to enjoy working in small groups with a wide variety of personalities, aptitudes, and attitudes toward science and teaching during the course of a semester.

A Couple of Samples

Consider the "snapshots" of two such self-paced exercises (Figures 4.1 and 4.2) from the author's own (Irwin, 1992) EE 316 lab/text.

The first activity provides preservice elementary teachers with practice in the more discriminating kinds of observation that they will encounter as they teach children from preschool through the middle grades. The second activity from the self-paced sequence in the author's methods course features an integration of more advanced science processes.

If your students find even one example or instance in which a marble of some color other than blue falls more slowly than the blue marble, then the hypothesis is disproved (not supported, negated) and must be reworded or rejected.

A little more background to chew on: To *disprove* a hypothesis takes only one observation that is contradictory to the hypothesis, while to *prove* a hypothesis requires a large number of cases be observed, all of which must support the hypothesis. Once all available cases have been observed and agree with the hypothesis, then it is said to be proven. In general then, it is usually easier to find one observation that negates a hypothesis than it is to make all possible observations and find they support it.

So, who cares? What's the big deal? Why should elementary students "give a flip" about hypotheses? Even though they are usually stated in broad, general terms, hypotheses are valuable because they are statements. Most of the knowledge humans have accumulated since the beginning of recorded history (and probably before that!) is the result of formulating general ideas and beliefs (hypotheses) and then changing and refining those ideas based on our experience and the experiences of others.

Your challenge as a teacher will be to guide students in setting up their tests, identifying relevant variables, defining terms and procedures. One good strategy for helping them but not telling them every step: Ask lots of leading questions. Questions guide them through the process of setting up an experiment but still preserve their "ownership" of it.

· Figure 4.1
Self-paced Activity #3

"Say What?": An Exercise in Communication

Objective: Upon completion of this exercise, you and your lab part-ner(s) will be able to describe the unique, observable characteris-tics of an object or organism that distinguishes it from similar objects/organisms in a set or group.

Materials Needed:
1. Matching locking plastic bags labeled C-1 and C-2, each con-taining 6-8 pieces of "Construx," Tinkertoys, or attribute blocks;
2. A set of 6-10 three-dimensional solids (cube, sphere, pyramid, cone, etc.);
3. "Packet Z": A locking plastic bag labeled "Packet Z," containing five miscellaneous common objects such as toy "jack," small rubber ball, unifix cube, empty medicine vial, marble, etc.;
4. File folder with a dozen or so different photocopies or overhead transparencies, each with images of sets of five common objects labeled ABCDE (examples: coins, paper clips, rubber bands, comb, pens, pencils, etc.).

The Main Activity:
In the kit of materials for Activity #3, you and your partner(s) will find two identical packets labeled C-1 and C-2, containing identical sets of attribute blocks, Tinkertoys, or plastic "Construx" pieces. For this first activity, work in pairs. (If there are three people in your group, the third person can be an "observer/recorder" and/or take turns with you or another partner. If there are four of you, form two pairs.) The paired partners take out all the toy pieces from packets C-1 and C-2. Make sure both sets have matching pieces. Then, seated back-to-back, without looking at each other, one of you assumes the role of "builder" and constructs some "arrangement" using four, five, or all of the attribute blocks, Tinkertoy, or Construx pieces.

Next, the "builder" describes, step-by-step, what he or she did to assemble his or her "masterpiece." At this point, the partner (the copier), who's been listening to these step-by-step directions from the builder, attempts to build an exact duplicate copy of the builder's assembly.

You may want to switch builder and copier roles and repeat this a time or two. Take time to talk about the clues, words, and phrases that did and did not help you succeed.

Another variation is to change the ground rules so that the builder signals when he or she has finished the construction, but says nothing; instead, the person playing the role of copier asks questions, to which the builder can only answer yes or no!

Answer these questions with your partner:
Did you experience any difficulties? What were they?

On repeated attempts, what kinds of things did you do to improve communication with each other?

What implications might this have for classroom teachers giving directions and sharing other forms of communication with elementary school students?

*   *   *   *

For the next activity, face your partner(s). Arrange the three-dimensional geometric solids from your kit on the table between you and your partners and play the old game "Information, Please!" The rules are simple:
1. You may only give one specific bit of information (one observable property) at a time.
2. Your partner(s) can only point to an object from the 3-D set if the information you give is sufficient to distinguish it from all others.
3. If your partner(s) cannot point to an object, he, she, or they say, "More information, please!" Then, you continue giving clues in the form of observable properties or characteristics until someone identifies your mystery object.

For example, you might say, "Look at the objects and select one that has a point on it." (Do they need more information?) If yes, give another clue; if no, they'll probably identify the object.

"Select one that has straight sides."
(Do they need more information?)
"Select one that has square corners."
(Do they need more information?)
Continue practicing this together with other objects in the room.

Practice Quiz: Write your responses to the tasks below on your own. You can talk about them with your partner(s) after everyone has finished.

Examine the objects in the locking plastic bag labeled "Packet Z," found in your Activity #3 kit. List only one or two observable characteristics needed to distinguish two objects from the others in the set.

Object_____

Characteristics_____

Object_____

Characteristics_____

Discussion of Practice Quiz: The key idea here is that the characteristic(s) or property(ies) you listed should be observable and should describe something unique about each object—something that distinguishes that object from the others in the set.

Talk to your partner(s) about this activity. If you still have doubts about your success, ask your instructor for help. This exercise is an important prerequisite to Activity #5, Classifying Things. So we want to make sure you feel comfortable with how you're describing objects before you try the"real quiz" for this activity.

Competency Check (The Real Quiz!) for Activity #3:
Find a file folder (near the kits of materials for self-paced tasks #3 and #5) with assorted drawings, photocopies, and overhead transparencies of sets of objects, labeled A B C D E. Select one of these sheets and examine the images of objects illustrated. In the spaces below, list the fewest observable properties necessary to distinguish each object from the others in the set.

A._____

B._____

C._____

D._____

E._____

Note: Show your instructor the responses you've written.
(There are so many possible acceptable descriptions, it is impractical to print a self-checking "answer key" for this activity.)

Figure 4.2
Self-Paced Activity #21

Testing Hypotheses

Objective: upon completion of this activity, you and your partner(s) will be able to design and describe a test for a hypothesis in terms of some experiment or new observations you could conduct to gain evidence to support or negate the hypothesis.

Materials Needed:
1. Falling Marble Demonstration: 3 capped medicine vials, each containing a liquid and a marble (marbles of a different color in each vial), all fastened together with two wooden strips across the tops and bottoms of the vials, held in place with masking tape (see Figure 1, below);
2. Several extra empty vials, wooden strips, masking tape;
3. A bottle of white corn syrup.

The Main Activity:
In the kit of materials labeled "Activity #21," find the Falling Marble device made from three medicine vials, each containing a liquid (water only, corn syrup only, and a mixture of 10% water and 90% corn syrup) and a marble, all fastened together with wooden strips taped across the tops and bottoms of the vials (see the illustration below).

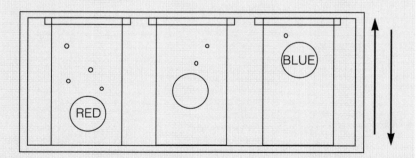

Hold the demonstration device so the vials are vertical and quickly, *flip it upside down!* Observe carefully. Try this a couple of times. Share thoughts and observations with your partner(s). Now, consider the statement below, made by some sixth graders after observing this same falling-marble system:

> Blue marbles fall through liquids more slowly than red marbles.

Talk this statement over with your partner(s), and then describe how you'd guide a group of sixth graders in testing (attempting to prove) this hypothesis.

Here's how you might have done it: Look at the students' original hypothesis. What attribute (variable) of the marbles does the statement suggest is influencing how fast marbles fall? (Color, right?) So, to test (prove/disprove, support/not support) their original hypothesis, they would need to compare the falling rates of *blue* marbles with the falling rates of marbles of *other colors*—the more different colors, the better—BUT, of matching weights and sizes. Why is it so important to match all other variables (keep them constant) when comparing the marbles and change only the color? (Talk this over with your partner(s). If you still have questions, ask your instructor for help.)

*   *   *   *

Here's a hypothesis that another team of sixth grade students wrote about the same falling-marble demonstration:

> Objects fall through "thin" liquids faster than "thick" liquids.

Discuss this one with your partner(s) and, in the space below, describe how you would guide students in setting up a test for this thin/thick liquid hypothesis.

Reflection on your ideas: As you and your partner(s) talked about this one, did you discuss the need for some kind of *operational definition* of thin and thick liquids? Perhaps any liquid as viscous as 90 percent corn syrup/10 percent water could be considered as thick. Conversely, any liquid that is less viscous than the 90/10 corn syrup-water solution might be described as "thin" or "thinner." Also, it would be important to use the same marble (or marbles identical in every observable way) to drop through liquids of many different thicknesses to give the hypothesis a thorough, valid test.

(Though this exercise is devoted to designing tests of hypotheses, there are extra vials, wooden strips, masking tape, and corn syrup in the kit for Activity #21 . . . if you have time and want to actually try a test of the above hypothesis, go for it! And, while you're at it, share your results and conclusions with classmates, maybe even with your instructor!)

Practice Quiz: Write your responses to the tasks below on your own. You can talk about them with your partner(s) after everyone has finished. Consider this hypothesis:

> By the end of the Phase I methods/observation semester, elementary education majors are more resistant to contagious diseases than students in any other academic major.

Describe what you'd do to test such a hypothesis.

Discussion of Practice Quiz: If you and your partner(s) suggested you'd have to establish some method for monitoring the health of a large sample of Phase I elementary education majors (perhaps by noting average number of absences from class due to illness) and compare your findings with data from majors in most, if not all other academic fields at the University, you're on the right track.

(If you still have questions or concerns about how you'd set up a test of any hypothesis, this is a good time to check in with Dr. Irwin and bounce your ideas off him, ask for clarification, etc.)

Competency Check for Activity #21:
As early as fourth grade, Peter Piper was growing pepper plants (for later picking and pickling!). As Peter and his favorite lab partner Polly spent those early years in intensive study, they observed some interesting things about the growth and development of pepper plants. In one series of experiments they planted pepper seeds in pretty rows of plastic pots. After a few weeks, some of the seedlings appeared green and vigorous, while others looked pale and puny. A few seeds didn't sprout at all.

Based on the above experience, Peter Piper and partner Polly proposed the following hypothesis about pepper plants:

Pepper plants need pretty purple plastic pots to produce palm-sized peppers.

Describe how you would test Peter and Polly's hypothesis.

As always, you can compare your response with the examples given in one of the self-checking Answer Keys available in the lab. (If you still have questions, check with your instructor for help.)

CONCLUSIONS

Because our elementary teacher candidates are placed in public school classrooms for two 3-week observation/teaching experiences during the Phase I methods semester, they have ample opportunities to use one or more of their self-paced science exercises as the basis for planning, teaching (with optional videotaping), and critiquing science lessons with children. In that observation/participation setting, they also observe their mentor teachers modeling various science process skills and teaching strategies, as well.

After tinkering with this small-group-centered, individually paced package of science methods activities continuously since 1969, we've accumulated enough pre-to-posttest gain score data and direct observations in the classroom to draw at least three conclusions:

First, employing hands-on activities adapted from current, developmentally appropriate, field-(school) tested science curricula ensures success in science for preservice elementary teacher candidates.

Second, packaging materials and structuring most activities in small cooperative/collaborative group settings creates a comfortable atmosphere, reduces most lingering traces of science anxiety, and enables students to embrace the "we're-all-in-this-together" feeling so that, sooner or later, those candidates take more risks in trying science experiences with children. And finally, because our students have enjoyed some honest success in science, and the confidence that builds with each small grain of success, they exhibit a greater willingness to endure the noise, mess, and time-consuming "hassle" of teaching child-centered, activity-based science during the student teaching semester and on into their teaching careers.

Supporting evidence: Some of the finest mentor teachers, with whom we are currently placing our Phase I students and our student teachers, were the Phase I science methods students of five, ten, and fifteen years ago. Something's RIGHT about this picture!

REFERENCES

Irwin, S. (1992). *Processes and Strategies for Engaging Children in Science.* Emporia, KS: Emporia State University Press.

————. (1994). *Course Syllabus: EE 316, Teaching Science in the Elementary School.* Emporia, KS: The Teachers College, Emporia State University.

Keith, R., & Thompson, K. (1994). *Course Syllabus: PS 115, Our Physical World.* Emporia, KS: Division of Physical Sciences, Emporia State University.

Robbins, L. (1994). *Course Syllabus: GB 303, Field and Lab Biology.* Emporia, KS: Division of Biological Sciences, Emporia State University.

5

THE USE OF GROUP INVESTIGATION IN HIGHER EDUCATION

by William G. Samuelson

Group investigation is a useful extension of and variation on the Cooperative Learning theme (Sharan & Sharan, 1992). Using group investigation with post-adolescents and adults in the university setting requires that the professor pay attention to the same concerns as teachers in the elementary grades or middle schools. Those concerns center around the planning that the teacher has to do to set up a group investigation in which the students can be successful and making sure that the students are ready or have the research and human relations skills necessary to conduct a successful group investigation.

Group Skills in Higher Education

Numerous theorists and practitioners in the field of Cooperative Learning have cited the need for the teacher to give students the opportunities to develop or practice the social, interactive, and collegial skills necessary for successful cooperative learning efforts. With all students in higher education, the professor risks making a strategic error if he or she assumes that because the students are post-secondary adults they know how to be contributing group members and how to operate in a group investigation. The best way to avoid making this error is to give students opportunities in the class to practice, review, or learn necessary skills by involving them in forms of Cooperative Learning (Think-Pair-Share, Numbered Heads Together, or Jigsaw). With some basic instruction, involvement in the processes of those strategies, and active teacher monitoring and assisting individual and group efforts, most college or university students can be prepared to use group investigation.

Many students in higher education classrooms have preferred learning styles that revolve around being solitary learners who are more comfortable in structured classroom settings learning from adult authority figures and using listening, note taking, and reading as primary avenues to learning new material. These skills have helped them survive academically. These students may be uncomfortable with Cooperative Learning and may not commit themselves to a group investigation if they do not have some opportunities to practice the skills of working together, discussing, mutual problem solving, reaching consensus, and encouraging or supporting each other during the investigative process. Thus, the more opportunities to use some sort of Cooperative Learning or group activity before branching out into group investigation, the better.

Planning for Group Investigation in Higher Education

The professor who wishes to use group investigation in the university classroom is likely to feel pressure to teach a specific amount of information in a certain time period. These time and curriculum pressures usually mean that the professor will not spend as much time preparing for a group investigation as a middle school or high school teacher might spend. University professors usually do not feel a need to contribute to the social development of their students and there is an implicit assumption by many that students already have the necessary skills. The best way to counteract such ideas is to do a good deal of specific planning and put much of it in the hands of students when the group investigation is begun. Directions and guidelines used by the group should be clearly stated and easy to understand—in fact some of the group processes can be taught through the directions or guidelines given to students.

Formation of Groups in Higher Education

Most writers on cooperation (such as Slavin, 1990 and Johnson & Johnson, 1994) acknowledge that heterogeneous groups provide the best mix for successful learning. In university classes, professors who use data cards filled out by the students can use that information to build groups in which students are distributed on the basis of grade point average, demonstrated ability in the class, major, gender, race, ethnic group, age, and/or social/fraternity membership. By observing students working in less structured and shorter-term Cooperative Learning strategies, the professor can assess the individuals in the class. Friendships or cliques can be identified that need to be divided during group assignments. Students can be observed who are shy or reticent and assign them to groups with nurturing members. Dominating or aggressive types of individuals can be noted so that feedback can be given before the group work and their early efforts can be monitored in the group investigation.

Stages of Implementation of Group Investigation

The professor needs to be aware of and plan for several stages in the development of a successful group investigation project for the class. Attention to these stages in planning and in implementation will help to assure satisfactory outcomes. Sharan (1990) identifies stages in the students' development of the group investigation project:

In planning and carrying out Group Investigation, pupils progress through a series of six consecutive stages. (It appears that adult learners will go through all of these stages in the production of their group investigation, but they may do some of them almost simultaneously.)

> *Stage One:* Identify the Topic and Organize the Groups
> *Stage Two:* Plan the Learning Task
> *Stage Three:* Carry Out the Investigation
> *Stage Four:* Summarize and Prepare the Final Report

Stage Five: Present the Final Report
Stage Six: Evaluate the Project, Student Achievement, and the Process.

The better the job that the professor does in preplanning the project and its guidelines, the more likely it will be that the students will produce a product that is appropriate to the class and that contributes to the course goals and objectives.

An Example of a Group Investigation

Population: Graduate students were in the course, Foundations of Education (Samuelson, 1988). All class members were certified and experienced teachers.

Overall Course Goal: Analyze the historical and contemporary state of major historical, social, and philosophic trends in U.S. society and education and make predictions based on that analysis.

Outcome Behavior: Identify significant events of major social, historical, and philosophic themes in U.S. education. Establish cause and effect relationships between and among the events that are selected to portray the theme. Predict outcomes of at least two currently operating events and predict two new elements that are likely to occur within the selected theme by the year 2025.

Logistics (Team Building)

After doing the initial planning, the students were divided into groups by the professor. The class was in the fourth week of a six-week summer course. On the first day of the fourth week, nine student leaders were identified by the professor around whom to build the groups (teams). During the first three weeks, these nine students had done the best work during class activities and on tests in which they demonstrated leadership, high achievement, and a grasp of the subject matter of the class. Other students were added to each team until all teams had three or four members. Because it was a summer session class with most of the students commuting to class, some care was exercised to build teams that carpooled, shared similar class schedules, or lived in town to facilitate working together outside of class time.

Selecting Topics

There was a need to provide instruction over specific topics judged by the professor to be essential information in the course. Because of time constraints, the professor chose to speed up the process usually identified under Stage One by letting the student groups choose the topic of their group investigation from a specified list of topics. After the teams were formed, they were instructed to pick three topics (from a list of thirteen topics) that all of the members of their team agreed were of at least some interest to them. They were asked to prioritize their choices from most to least desirable. After all teams were finished with their task of selecting three topics, the professor assigned each group a number and then drawing random numbers (one through nine) allowed each team to state a choice of topic. If the first choice for the second team was selected by the first team, the second team received their second choice. This continued until all teams had chosen topics. Because there were five more topics than teams, it worked out that every team received one of their first three choices.

Topic Choices
A partial list of topics includes:
- The development of secondary education in the United States
- The development of elementary schools in the United States.
- The development of education in Kansas from the 1830s
- The development of the role(s) of females in U.S. schools

- The development of recruitment, training, and certi-
fication of teachers since 1620.
- The development of the education of minorities in
the United States.

When each team had selected a topic, it received the
guidelines for how the project was to be completed and the
nature of the final report.

GUIDELINES FOR THE GROUP INVESTIGATION
Historical Trend Analysis

Complete the assignment by following this list of procedures:

All team members are to gather data that can be used in
fulfilling the following final report assignment. (All team members
are to be equitably involved in research of the topic and in the
final presentation. Specific roles and tasks may be assigned within
the team to facilitate the team efforts as long as roles are equitably
assigned or assumed.) These are activities normally accomplished
in *Stage One*.

The team members shall decide the elements of the project. They will assign tasks and divide responsibilities equitably
among team members. They will stablish a time table for data
gathering, for decision making, and for planning the presentation.
(Stage Two)

The team will plan to make a class presentation (final
report) of a list of no less than 15 and no more than 20 significant
events in the development of a trend (or trends) in the selected
topic. Each member is to develop an individual list of 10 to 15
events from which the group will develop a consensus list of 15
to 20 of the most important events. (Individual lists will be hand-
ed in to the professor when the consensus list has been com-
piled.) Group members will be expected to establish a rationale
for the inclusion and exclusion of each item rather than just
accept events that are on all individual member's lists. *(Stage Two/
Stage Three)*

As the team members are researching, they are compiling
a bibliography of resources that they have consulted. This bibliog-

raphy will be submitted to the professor when the report is given. *(Stage Two)*

The team will then identify two of the currently operating events of the trend or topic and predict how they believe those events will play out and affect the future direction of this trend as it relates to their chosen topic. These are activities normally found in *Stage Three* and *Stage Four.*

The team will also predict two events that they believe will (or conceivably could) happen and that will (could) continue to influence this trend (topic) in the future up to the year 2025. *(Stage Four)*

The team will provide classmates with a hand-out of no more than two pages to help them prepare for a test over the project. *(Stage Four)*

The team will develop and provide a time line to help classmates develop a sense of historical perspective regarding the selected topic. *(Stage Four)*

The team will plan a final report whose presentation will involve all members of the class during some part of the presentation. *(Stage Four)*

The team should plan to use at least one visual aid to assist classmates in understanding their report. *(Stage Four)*

The team should plan to make use of excellent teaching skills in developing the final report on their selected topic. Each member of a team must use some technique or strategy during his or her presentation so that it is different from that of other members. *(Stage Four)*

The final report may take up to thirty minutes; therefore time distribution among team members during the report should be carefully planned and monitored. *(Stage Four)*

The team will develop a list of four higher-order thinking skills questions about the topic of their presentation. Those questions will be submitted to the professor, and one of those questions will be used on the exam covering this section of the course. This planning effort by the team in *Stage Four* is used in *Stage Six.*

THE FINAL REPORTS
Stage Five: Present the Final Report

The teams had approximately two weeks to prepare for the presentation of their final reports, which were given in the last week of the course. Two or three reports were given each day (class periods for the summer course were 2 hours and 50 minutes long). At the end of each report there were ten minutes for the other classmates and the professor to ask the reporting team questions for clarification or extension. Also, there was time at the conclusion of each report for the professor to add events of importance that had been inadvertently omitted, to amplify elements that were inadequately covered, or to correct misleading information.

EVALUATION OF THE FINAL REPORTS
Stage Six: Evaluate the Project, Student Achievement, and the Process

The group work and the final projects were evaluated in the following way. Each group member wrote a half-page narrative report of the work of the other members of the group. They did not comment on their own work. Each group member wrote a half-page report about the most important thing(s) that they learned from working in a group on this topic. The professor read and evaluated those two assignments. The professor rated or evaluated the portion of the presentation done by the group as a whole and by each member individually. The students listening to the report evaluated the report on five variables: (1) Did it keep your attention? (2) Did it present new information? (3) Did the presentation make the information easy to remember and understand? (4) How useful were the accompanying handouts? (5) How well did the report and handouts seem to fulfill the guidelines?

This process of evaluation resulted in quantitative and qualitative data reflecting four variables: (1) a view of the individual by the other members of the group, (2) a self-report by the individual, (3) the professor's evaluation of the quality of the individual member's portion of the report and the report as a whole, and (4) student perspectives on the report and handout materials. The grade for the group investigation counted 20 percent of the total course grade.

ROLE OF THE PROFESSOR

The role of the professor during a group investigation is different from the role of a professor during a lecture presentation. The following professor's tasks provide information about some of that difference:

1. Developed (identified) the range of topics for student selection.
2. Developed the guidelines for conducting the study and the presentation of the report.
3. Selected the membership of the groups.
4. Monitored group processes during the investigation activities that took place during class time (focusing on cooperative skills).
5. Facilitated the development of the content of the final report (answered questions, asked questions, made suggestions, gave assistance where needed, helped get groups moving that had gotten "stuck").
6. Evaluated the individual and group final reports based on observed group work and final presentation.
7. Gave feedback and corrective information (when, if necessary).
8. Read the evaluations of individuals, team peers, and other non-team classmates.
9. Assigned grades to individual team members.

REFERENCES

Johnson, D. W., & Johnson, R. T. (1994). *Learning Together and Alone: Cooperative, Competitive, and Individualistic Learning.* 4th ed. Boston: Allyn and Bacon.

Samuelson, W. (1988). *Shaping American Education.* Emporia, KS: Emporia State University Press.

Sharan, Y. (1990). "Group Investigation: Expanding Cooperative Learning." In M. P. Brubacher Ryder, Rickett, and Kemp, eds., *Perspectives on Small Group Planning: Theory and Practice.* Oakville, Ontario: Rubicon Publishing.

Sharan, Y. S., & Sharan, S. (1992). *Expanding Cooperative Learning Through Group Investigation.* New York: Teachers College Press.

Slavin, R. E. (1990). Cooperative Learning: Theory, Research, and Practice. Englewood Cliffs, NJ: Prentice Hall.

6

COOPERATIVE LEARNING AND MATHEMATICS EDUCATION

by Jean Morrow

Introduction

Most of us are familiar with the adage "We teach as we've been taught." Most of us wish that our preservice students would "teach as they've been taught to teach." But wishing, I've learned, won't necessarily make it so. Consequently, as I studied a working draft of the *Curriculum and Evaluation Standards for School Mathematics* (1990), published by the National Council of Teachers of Mathematics (NCTM) (five months before I began teaching mathematics methods for elementary and middle school teachers at Emporia State University), I realized that I would have to incorporate new strategies into my own instruction. I began with a Cooperative Learning approach to lesson planning, and eventually broadened the scope of Cooperative Learning activities to include the final exam.

Get It Together

The first day of class I introduce the idea of cooperative groups by using the activity "Build It" from the book *Get It Together (Math Problems for Groups, Grades 4-12)*, by Ericson (1989). Students are divided into teams of four and are given a series of five sets of clues and a set of 13 colored blocks. Each person is to share the information gleaned from his or her clue without simply reading the clue to the rest of the group, or handing it to someone in the group to "figure it out."

Students usually employ some problem-solving strategies such as determining whether or not a given clue is an appropriate one with which to begin. Sharing the information contained in their clues eventually enables the group to determine which six of the blocks and what type of arrangement is needed in order to satisfy all of the clues simultaneously for any given set. There is generally lively discussion within the group about the meanings of such terms as *above, face, edge,* and *between.* The class ends with a debriefing session on events and reactions during the "Build It" activities.

Lesson Planning

During the next class session, I propose the Cooperative Learning activities related to the topics assigned in the syllabus. The final activity for each topic consists of four parts—journal readings, lesson plan, learning center, and assessment. The journal readings (a minimum of two articles) are the input for the lesson plan and the learning center or the assessment. The learning center and the assessment must be aligned with the objectives and activities of the lesson plan. The group must do an oral presentation to the class and submit a written copy to me. Three groups are assigned to the same topic but a different grade level: one prepares a K-2 lesson; one, a 3-5 lesson; and one, a 6-8 lesson. The grade level assignment changes with each topic. Over the course of the semester, each group will present on five topics.

Students are asked to submit a list of up to four names, if they have a preference as to members in their group. Anyone who expresses no preference will be assigned to a group by me. Group membership remains the same throughout the semester. If the number in the class is such that some groups are comprised of five students, a second learning center is developed.

At the beginning of each semester there is generally some resistance to the Cooperative Learning arrangement—"I don't want my grade lowered because someone doesn't do their part." I address this issue by assigning an analytical (individual piece) and holistic (the entire project) grade to the project so that each student has two grades. In eight semesters of grading in this manner, no student has earned a lower grade because of the holistic ratings included in the overall evaluation.

When students work together, their first project usually lacks one of the basic elements for Cooperative Learning described by Johnson and Johnson (1994)—namely, face-to-face interaction. The group meets, determines a topic (e.g., linear measurement), assigns roles, and meets again the morning of the class presentation. As can be expected, there is little if any alignment among the various components in the first project, which usually deals with the teaching of geometry. Typically, the articles concern shapes or area and perimeter, the lesson plan deals with nonstandard measurement, the learning center is an estimation activity, and the assessment involves measuring with a metric ruler. Such an obvious demonstration of nonalignment, and the discussion of the importance of planning together, lead to better results in later projects.

Cooperative Teaching

At least one of the sections will have an opportunity to revisit the teaching of geometry when we have a "teach-in" with the physical education methods class. Kathy Ermler, a professor of physical education, and I each divide our classes into three groups and assign each to a primary, intermediate, or junior high level. The mathematics methods students prepare a classroom activity to teach a particular concept. The physical education majors prepare a physical movement activity that also incorporates that concept. We meet for a two-hour period, with the mathematics methods students using the first hour for teaching; and the physical education majors, the second hour. Each teaching station lasts 12-15 minutes, with a 5-minute debriefing session at the end. Typically, the primary group focuses on geometric shapes; the intermediate group, volume and capacity; and the junior high group, angle measurement and orienteering. At the end, we bring both groups together for a summary evaluation, and suggestions for improvements. Each class learns much from the other.

To prepare for this "teach-in," the students have an opportunity to practice in a cooperative group setting as they revise plans, determine who will present what portion of the lesson and who will prepare materials. If the group does not work together in their planning, they hear about it not once but three times—as each new group rotates through their section on the day of the "teach-in."

A Cooperative Final

During my third year of teaching the elementary and middle school mathematics methods, I asked the students what they would think of a final exam that consisted of two parts—a cooperative group portion and an individual response essay. For the cooperative group portion, students would be able to use their textbooks, notes, and other resources (e. g., calculators and manipulatives). The essay would be a solo effort with no outside resources permitted. I was more than a little surprised with how readily they agreed to try this new testing arrangement.

To be perfectly honest, I had visions of students dividing up the questions and simply rattling off answers to one another near the end of the 90 minutes allotted. I did encourage the students to form groups so that at least two different textbook resources were available. (Students had a choice of any one of four textbooks for the methods course, since I wanted a variety of resources and approaches available.) I also encouraged them to use a jigsaw-type approach—with each student in the group concentrating on just two or three areas contained on the final exam.

Since all three sections of students took the test at the same time, I also encouraged students from different sections to work together. Each student turned in his or her own test, so that if there was strong disagreement within the group about an appropriate response, the individual student could make his or her own choice. As I circulated around the room during that first trial of the cooperative group test, I was elated to hear thoughtful discussion and probing questions as students listened to the "expert" and then brought their own knowledge and experience to bear on the situation. I continued to use this approach for the next three semesters and was not once disappointed by the students' attitude and participation in this final activity.

Distance Learning and Cooperative Learning

After three semesters of working with my undergraduate students, I had an opportunity to teach in a distance learning situation. I was offering a class on implementing the NCTM Standards (National Council of Teachers of Mathematics, 1990) for in-service teachers. Two class sessions, the opening and closing, would be aired over satellite with two-way audio, one-way video. The remaining sessions would involve viewing videotapes, and working activities with a small group. The value of working with a small group was so important to me, that we did not permit a site to host the class unless there were at least three students in the class. There were to be three nights during the semester when we would have a conference-call class (Telenet). I made a site visit to each of the seven sites hosting the class once during the semester for a face-to-face meeting with the students there.

In the opening satellite broadcast each site was assigned a question related to aspects of teaching and implementing problem solving. At the site, the teachers were to brainstorm answers, select a spokesperson, and report to the entire group at the appropriate time. The purpose of this first activity was twofold—to give the participants at each site an opportunity to converse about mathematics teaching and to provide a situation in which they would have to "use" the technology.

The activity book for the course was structured in a way that enabled the participants to investigate, explore, look for patterns, seek to generalize results, and develop classroom approaches. Since many of the teachers were looking at new concepts and strategies, the importance of group support and interaction could not be overlooked. Although not all activities were true

Cooperative Learning situations, several did require that setting.

One activity that was a cooperative group problem is called "Place Your Shape." Each group has five plane figure shapes—a square, a triangle, a hexagon, a trapezoid, and a rhombus (not a square). Most elementary school teachers are familiar with these pieces as manipulatives from the "Pattern Blocks." Four clues are provided to help the group place their pieces in a horizontal grid. Once teachers have successfully completed the two puzzles provided, they are asked to write a new set of clues that others in the class can attempt to follow. Many teachers in fact do this very type of activity with their own students, but they have rarely had the experience of doing it themselves.

Over the next two semesters, this course was repeated and a second course in alternative assessment in mathematics was also offered. The use of "think-pair-share" and jigsaw strategies were important elements of the course. A combination of these techniques is used in the activity that introduces patterns that lead to functions—an extension of patterns into the realm of algebra for elementary school teachers. We begin with a whole class activity that involves solving two problems:

> 1. Suppose you have 25 counters and 2 containers. How many ways could you put the 25 counters into the 2 containers?

> 2. Suppose everyone in this class were to shake hands with every other person in the class. How many handshakes would that be?

These two problems involve similar approaches in arriving at a solution. Once we developed the idea of "making it simpler" and using a table, we started with 1 counter or 1 person, then 2, 3, and so on. We described the patterns we saw and tried to predict the answer for, say 30 counters or 50 people. Then the teachers were given one of six related experiments and asked to find the solution and describe the pattern. After some time for individual work, all those who had the same experiment got together and compared results. New groups were formed with one person with each experiment in the new group. They shared their problem, their approach, and their solution. Finally, the group was asked to work together to find a common thread, a generalization that might apply to any problems of this type. They were asked, as well, to find an expression for the "nth" event—whether that would be the 10th, the 50th, or the 999th one. For many of the elementary teachers in these classes, this is one of the first in-depth mathematical discussions in which they have participated since beginning their teaching career. They have talked often, and at length, about teaching mathematics, but many have not studied mathematics since their sophomore year in college. The Cooperative Learning environment is supportive and less threatening, enabling them to push the limits of their own experience.

Finally, I had an opportunity to offer a class over a fiber-optic interactive television network. We originally had four sites, three remote and the one from which I was broadcasting. On the first night there was only one student at one site and so she was encouraged to go to another site that was just a 15-minute drive from her first site. Again, the use of cooperative groups at each site was an important component of the class. This particular setting gave us an opportunity to explore cooperative group activities in which not all the participants of the group were at the same site. For instance, Site A had seven teachers; Site B, nine; Site C, fourteen. One activity had two teachers from Site A paired with two teachers from Site C. Another time, one teacher from Site A, three from Site B, and two from Site C joined together. The advantages to the cross-site grouping included the opportunity for teachers from different schools and districts to work together and share mathematical learning. The disadvantages were linked more to the technology—the group conferring over the network could be a distraction. In order for them to see each other's work, they made use of "ELMO"—which displayed their work for anyone and everyone to see. Two activities that worked well included a numerical variation of "Place Your Shape" called "Build a Number" and the game, "Phooey!"

"Build a Number" requires each member of the group to have a set of number tiles from 0 to 9, and a set of clues.

Each group member gets one clue and proceeds to build a number that satisfies the condition in his or her clue. When all students are finished, each shares his or her number and clue with the group. Then the group works together to find one number that satisfies all the conditions simultaneously.

"Phooey!" is a place value game that can be played competitively or cooperatively. Each group needs a set of 6 number cubes (more or less depending on the knowledge base of the students playing the game) and a recording sheet. I generally limit this sheet to twelve lines (i.e., a half sheet of paper). The first person rolls the six number cubes and makes the largest number possible. That number is written on the top line. The next person rolls the six number cubes and makes the smallest number possible. That number is written on the bottom line. Now, every number formed after that must fit between the recorded numbers—one number per line. In the competitive version, students try to place their numbers so as to make it as difficult as possible for the next player. If a player cannot place a number, he or she says, "Phooey!" and is out of the game for the remainder of that round. In the cooperative version, the focus is on every student being able to put a number in the list. Even in the cooperative version, however, a student must occasionally declare "Phooey!"

Advantages

For many of my undergraduate students these are their first experiences with Cooperative Learning. For some of my graduate students this is also their first experience with Cooperative Learning, particularly in mathematics. Many of them have done small-group work in high school and university classes, but rarely Cooperative Learning.

The methods experience has at least two benefits from my perspective: (1) Preservice teachers develop expertise in the roles and expectations of Cooperative Learning by participating in a series of five or six projects, which gives them a comfort level that will permit them to use this strategy in their own classrooms in another year or so. (2) The students have an opportunity to plan with peer professionals-in-training, which provides a model for working with peers in a school setting, so that students won't feel the need to walk into their first classroom and hang a "Do Not Disturb" sign on their classroom door.

The use of cooperative groups in my distance learning classes also has at least two benefits: (1) There is a level of interaction that is not typical of many TV courses. (2) The cooperative grouping provides a risk-free zone for teachers to explore concepts in algebra, geometry, statistics, and probability that expand their understanding of the mathematics contained within a given activity or game. In either situation, I believe that Cooperative Learning activities are a vital element if we are to make the shift in the environment of mathematics classrooms called for in the National Council of Teachers of Mathematics (1991) document, *Professional Standards for Teaching Mathematics:* (see p. 3,) "Toward classrooms as mathematical communities—away from classrooms as simply a collection of individuals."

REFERENCES

Ericson, T. (1989). *Get It Together.* EQUALS. Lawrence Hall of Science. Berkeley: University of California.

Johnson, D.W., & Johnson, R.T. (1994). *Learning Together and Alone: Cooperative, Competitive, and Individualistic Learning.* 4th ed. Boston: Allyn and Bacon.

National Council of Teachers of Mathematics. (1990). *Curriculum and Evaluation Standards for School Mathematics.* Reston, VA.: The Council.

———. (1991). *Professional Standards for Teaching Mathematics.* Reston, VA.: The Council.

7

LEARNING TOGETHER IN MATHEMATICS

by Connie S. Schrock

Cooperative Learning and mathematics are natural partners. In order to learn mathematics students must do mathematics. Often learning mathematics can be a difficult task if done independently. Students who are learning calculus or other college level mathematics are often at a loss of where to begin or become confused before they finish an assignment or problem. Often the cause is waiting too long to begin work. Material from the lesson that seemed so clear in class is no longer fresh in their minds and key points have been forgotten. For that reason, students should be encouraged to work as soon after the class period as possible. Also students should be encouraged to seek out a study group. Working with others gives students face-to-face interaction and a positive interdependence necessary to learn and successfully complete tasks.

Finding and properly using a study group is not an easy project for many students. Classroom cooperative groups can facilitate this process. In most of my introductory-level classes, building classroom pairs are established as a first step toward cooperative groups. Students are paired in class and arranged around the room so that one of the partners is at the chalkboard. The second student is seated next to his or her partner. Problems are presented to the class orally. A sample problem might be: Find the first derivative given the function, $f(x) = (x2 + 5x - 3)(\sin x)$. One partner works at the board while the other is seated to work the problem on paper. The students working together and help each other understand the problem. This technique allows the instructor to scan all board work to determine student progress and levels of understanding. The instructor can then help students who are struggling and can increase the level of difficulty at the appro-

94

priate pace. Students are asked to trade places so that both partners will have experience in each role. At the conclusion of the lesson each pair will have one complete set of notes and correctly worked problems. This can facilitate further study and collaboration to share notes. Initially, you may use a random process for pairing. As you get to know your class and each student's abilities, it is appropriate to change the pairing each time. This will help students get to know each other and begin to communicate openly with each other.

Another way this technique may be used is to introduce material using a discovery approach. For example, given that the students know how to find the first derivative and critical values, they can use a graphics calculator and well-structured problems to discover the First Derivative Test. The seated student graphs the functions while his or her partner finds the first derivative and the critical values at the board. Students are then guided to place critical values on a number line and to evaluate the sign on each interval. The instructor can easily look around the room and give appropriate guidance when needed. To complete the lesson, each pair of students is grouped with another pair and asked to summarize how to determine whether a critical number is a local maximum, local minimum, or not a local extreme value. A good sequence of problems might include the following:

a. $f(x) = x2 - 5x + 3$
b. $f(x) = -x2 + 2x - 4$
c. $f(x) = -x3 + x - 4$
d. $f(x) = x3$
e. $f(x) = 3x4 - 4x3 - 12x2 + 5$
f. $f(x) = x4 - x$
g. $f(x) = x3 (x-3)2$

By working together, students practice necessary skills and are able to talk about mathematics.

Another effective use of this board pairs technique is as a review for a test or chapter. Students require study notes, and they often prefer to watch someone else work problems. This does not allow the instructor to locate the students' trouble areas as easily, nor does it provide the needed practice before the examination. Therefore, by using the board pairs, students practice and learn, as well as have a set of notes to study. After students become familiar with this technique, they often ask to use it in class.

As students become comfortable working with each other and the instructor, the instructor should form heterogeneous groups of four students. Problem-solving projects that apply the mathematics are excellent choices for group assignments. At the college level many roles emerge in the process of doing a group assignment. Often the only role that needs to be assigned is that of the group leader. Students are usually allowed to decide within their groups who will fulfill the remaining roles. Some roles that emerge are recorder, facilitator, accuracy checker, researcher, and encourager.

One project that generated much interest in calculus was to design a roller coaster.

You have been hired by Emporia's amusement park, Dorothy and Toto's Playground, to design the new roller coaster ride, Terrific Twister. Your committee must design the up and down path for a 400-meter straight stretch. Your paper should be written so that the amusement park management can understand it. Include at least two designs, one that you believe to be the most exciting and one that uses the least amount of material for supports. Be sure to explain where the coaster is decreasing at an increasing rate, decreasing at a decreasing rate, increasing at an increasing rate, or increasing at a decreasing rate. Show how you have considered safety, the course graphs, slope, and rate of change of slope. Below is a list of the rules given to you by the amusement park management.

1. The angle of the descent that the path makes with a horizontal can be no steeper than 75° at any point.

2. There must be a support beam every 20 meters.

3. The amount of material needed for a support beam is the square of its length.

4. The first incline on the path is 50°.

5. Thrill is defined to be the sum of the radian measures of the angle at the steepest descent for each fall plus the number of peaks.

For this project students are assigned to groups of three or four with a group leader. The group leader is responsible for assigning duties, keeping the project moving, and submitting the completed report on time. Projects of this type demonstrate what the students know and comprehend. They provide an authentic assessment of student learning.

Using a Cooperative Learning approach to this lesson gives students the opportunity to talk about mathematics, to experience a variety of approaches to an open-ended problem, and to share the responsibilities with others. Asking the students to work alone on projects of this type usually produces weaker or incomplete papers.

One of the drawbacks to Cooperative Learning of this type involves grading. Often the more gifted or well-prepared students have some difficulty with group assignments, especially if the individual student believes that he or she could have been more successful working the task alone. One way to deal with this problem is to continue to give one project grade but to allow each student to submit a brief evaluation. This evaluation is confidential and is not returned. Ask each student to assign a percentage that represents the amount of work he or she believes was contributed by each group member. Require the evaluation percentages to total 100 percent. For example:

Name of evaluator:	Mary	% Work _____
Group members:	Ted	% Work _____
	Quincy	% Work _____
	Maria	% Work _____
	Total	100%

The student may add any comments that he or she feels is necessary. Another valuable question that should be asked is "What did you learn on this assignment?" Most students are open and honest with these assessments. For example, unless there is a major problem within a group, Mary would get approximately the same percent from all four individual's evaluations. The process of submitting these reports, even if it does not change an individual's grade, allows students to provide input and helps to alleviate the stress some students feel from group grading.

Another step that benefits students is rotating the leadership role in the group. It is not as important to assign the best student as group leader as it is to allow each individual to experience that role. Many students rise to the challenge. Students who seek leadership roles also benefit from a different role within the group.

A most important step is to share your objectives and reasoning with your students. One student wrote on an end of the semester evaluation that he or she had learned much more from his or her peers than from the instructor. Although the student may have intended it to be a negative comment, it was a valuable one and it let the instructor know that the Cooperative Learning was working. Had the student been aware of the instructor's goal for learning he or she may have written the same comment, but it would have been intended as a positive comment.

Another good group activity involves the use of a Computer Algebra System and calculus problems that are more realistic. By using a computer tool, students can work problems that are not contrived to have nice numbers for easier calculation. For example:

> Tornado Contracting Company (T.C.C.) is bidding on a contract to make rectangular troughs. These are open containers with square bases and made of a material that costs $8.50 per square meter. The sides are made of a less expensive alloy that costs $4.65 per square meter. The contractor must assemble the trough by welding the seams together at a cost of $3.95 per meter. This cost includes all overhead. The client wants each box to hold 2,340 cubic meters. What dimensions should the company propose to ensure the lowest costs? If T.C.C. wishes to make 18 percent profit based on their cost, what would be the bid to make 750 troughs? Write up your bid as you would present it to your company president.

Another role emerges from projects of this type, that of the technician. The technician has the primary responsibility for running the computer and using it to calculate solutions. Students must understand the concepts and the problem in order to create the equations for the technician to use. The next step involves interpreting the values obtained through the use of the computer. Finally, the group must write up the problem and explain it so that the company president can understand it.

In the History of Mathematics (MA 460) course, there is another activity that can help students learn together. Students are told that on the required date they must be familiar with a group of mathematicians for a quiz. The instructor states that it is an unusual type of a quiz, and it will not follow the traditional format. The students are also told that the quiz will involve some work within their cooperative groups of 4 or 5 students. When class begins on the designated date each group is given one set of the following directions:

> Your group is to create a quiz over the specified mathematicians. Work as a group. Remember you may need to divide responsibilities in order to complete the assignment in the 30 minutes you are allowed for this part of the task. You may use your textbook and class notes. The answer key should be written on a paper separate from the quiz. Each of the 22 mathematicians on your list must be covered on the quiz. You must include 5 fill-in-the-blank questions, 6 matching questions, 3 multiple-choice questions, 2 short-answer questions, 1 essay question, and 1 open-ended question. The remainder of the necessary questions may be of any type that your group selects.

> At the end of 30 minutes your group will submit your papers. The instructor will then give you a quiz written by another group to complete. During the second part of class you will not be allowed to use notes or your book. The members of your group will work together. Your grade will be a combination of the quiz you create and the quiz that you complete.

It is important to continue to monitor groups, answer questions, and make sure that the students understand the task. When grading, look at the questions created to make sure that they are clear and can be answered. Next, check the submitted answer keys for clarity and correctness. Finally, grade the completed tests. One combined score is then given to each group. During the next class period it is important to have a discussion with the students about the entire process. Students need to recognize how much they achieved during the process. It is important to point out that more learning transpired, because the students could collaborate, communicate, and continue to learn as they created their quiz. Individual accountability can then be measured by a traditional exam during the next grading period.

For teacher preparation, it is crucial that students learn to work with each other productively. Regardless of a student's personal preference for learning, collaboration is a needed life skill. The National Council of Teachers of Mathematics (1989) supports Cooperative Learning experiences in its *Curriculum and Evaluation Standards for School Mathematics.* It states that when teaching school mathematics, teachers should incorporate Cooperative Learning activities as much as possible in daily classroom activities. Students in the Teaching Secondary Mathematics (MA 470) course work together throughout the course. During the entire semester the students watch and take turns teaching trigonometry. The students teach once individually and again as a part of a team. The team's teaching is an open-ended task for which the group must plan and complete the task in the best way possible. The team must keep in mind the subject material assigned and how to provide for the most effective learning for the students enrolled in trigonometry. It is a challenge to blend many different personalities into one presentation or even to select the most important course of action.

Another important group project completed in this course is to write, administer, and grade an examination for the College Trigonometry class. This authentic task allows students to see how questions are answered, which questions were not as clearly worded as they needed to be, and how to plan for time constraints. For these two tasks, no roles are assigned. Much can be learned about your students by watching the roles emerge within the group. Since these projects are completed outside of class time, new difficulties can arise. Students have to manage outside time constraints, schedules, and a variety of dispositions toward tasks. Students who normally procrastinate might be in a group with early planners and interpersonal skills are essential. An assessment sheet, as previously described, is beneficial for these projects.

In some courses it is important to have students do original work or experiments. Cooperative groups can facilitate this work. One of the courses for which this is a natural activity is Probability and Statistics (MA 380). A problem that generated great interest is the following one:

Find the correct length to cut a paper towel roll cylinder so that if it is dropped from 3 feet it will have the same probability of landing on its end as it does of landing on the cardboard surface.

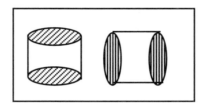

Working on the problem together helped the students set up and approach the problem. It is much more fun to experiment when one is not working alone. The same is true for a course like Mathematical Modeling (MA 291). Students must experiment and model situations in order to begin to understand the subject. Group projects can be very exciting when students are left to create their own modeling project.

A colleague of mine, Joe Yanik, has students work in cooperative groups to determine if given conjectures are true. For Abstract Algebra (MA 425), he provides students with the following directions:

Each of the following statements will appear, in one form or another, on Exam II. It is up to your group to determine whether each of them is, in general, true or false. Prove those that are true and find a specific counter-example for those that are false.

In each of the following conjectures G is a group and H is a subgroup of G.
   1. S_5 has no subgroup of order 6.
   2. If K is a subgroup of H, then K is a subgroup of G.
   3. If H has even order, then G has even order.

Three examples are given, but this list might contain as many as 15 conjectures. The groups again are necessary for students to be successful. Having other students to collaborate with is necessary to keep students from becoming discouraged and giving up long before results are produced. Individual accountability is maintained by the course examinations. Students in groups that develop good communication and collaboration skills perform well on the individual assessments.

This same technique can be used in other lower-level courses as well. Students would still be asked if a conjecture is true or false but not asked to prove it. They should provide counter examples. For example, in a calculus class here are some conjectures that may be used.

1. For a given function $y=f(x)$ if we know that $f(2)=0$, then it is always true that $f'(2)=0$.

2. A tangent line to the graph of a function will always intersect the graph in only one place.

3. For a given function $y=f(x)$, if we know that $f(x)>0$ for all x such that $1 \leq x \leq 2$, then it is always true that $f(2) > f(1)$.

Student attitudes and achievements can be facilitated through the use of Cooperative Learning groups in mathematics, as well as other subjects. Team-building exercises will help to create a supportive environment in which to learn. Understanding is enhanced when an appropriate task is selected and clearly explained. Instructors must also explain the expected goals and learning objectives. Individual accountability should be ensured through multiple assessments. The National Council of Teachers of Mathematics (1991) report, *Professional Standards for Teaching Mathematics*, points out that teachers are influenced by the teaching that they see and experience. Teachers who are expected to use Cooperative Learning must use and experience it throughout their professional development. The Mathematical Association of America (1991) encourages all teachers of collegiate mathematics to think deeply about how we teach as well as what we teach each time we prepare to teach a course.

REFERENCES

Mathematical Association of America. (1991). *A Call for Change: Recommendations for the Mathematical Preparation of Teachers of Mathematics. Committee on the Mathematical Education of Teachers.* James R. C. Leitzel, editor. Washington, D. C.

National Council of Teachers of Mathematics. (1989). *Curriculum and Evaluation Standards for School Mathematics.* Reston, VA: The Council.

―――. (1991). *Professional Standards for Teaching Mathematics.* Reston, VA: The Council.

8

READING CLASSES AND COOPERATIVE LEARNING

by Joanne M. Larson

When teaching reading methods courses to preservice teachers, I often use Cooperative Learning groups. This approach not only helps students learn about Cooperative Learning, but also it helps them as future educators. In fact, students experience how learning occurs when they work with their peers. Another reason I use Cooperative Learning is that it stimulates class discussion—students are more willing to actively participate in class discussion if they have been placed in situations where they can first discuss the content with several classmates. Over the years I have learned several strategies that help my Cooperative Learning groups become more effective.

Starting the Semester

Early in the semester, I like to use the Think-Pair-Share approach for several reasons. The students in the class are just beginning to know one another. Think-Pair-Share helps students learn about each other on a one-on-one basis. When preservice teachers discuss a topic with a partner, they not only learn more about the topic and ask better questions, but they also learn about one another. This approach enhances the building of a community of students in the classroom, which leads to student willingness to take risks and state opinions with classmates they've come to know. It's not unusual for one student to speak for another, such as, "Well, Jenny had a great idea . . ." This form of communication contributes to the strong sense of community among students in the class.

During one session in an elementary literacy course, the class discussed reading comprehension. I divided the group into pairs of students and asked them to determine what "reading comprehension" meant and to generate a list of reasons why some texts were easier to read than others. The preservice teachers brainstormed in pairs for about three minutes. Next, I called on each pair to offer an item from their list. These items were written on the board:

> length of text
> size of print
> illustrations
> interest in subject
> date text was written
> author
> writer's style
> reason for reading text

After we created the list, I asked the students to consider which items would most likely influence reading comprehension. The students ranked them accordingly. These responses were then used to initiate a discussion of their search regarding comprehension.

Class discussions that were introduced through the Think-Pair-Share approach enhanced interest and enthusiasm, because all students participated. The students contributed directly to the topic while brainstorming with partners and listing ideas on the board. They contributed to their own learning as they recognized items that they had discussed with their partner being cited by their classmates.

Short Projects

Sometimes, I have preservice teachers working cooperative groups to complete short, in-class miniprojects. Because many of my students are experiencing Cooperative Learning for the first time, they rely heavily on a description I give them as a handout (see Figure 8.1). The miniproject handout includes specific descriptions of the cooperative roles for students, instructions for the task to be accomplished, and time guidelines for completing the assignment in class. In short, the handout serves as a reference while students develop their project.

For example, after studying a variety of prereading strategies, I decided to have my university students create a Problematic Situation using the text "I Have A Dream" by Martin

Figure 8.1
CI 416: Reading in the Secondary Schools

Cooperative Group Project:
Creating a Problematic Situation Using the Text
"I Have A Dream"

Group Members
Timer:_____
(Time the group's two activities: (1) spend 4 minutes discussing what concepts could be used and (2) choose one of the concepts to use and spend 10 minutes developing a Problematic Situation.)

Recorder:_____
(Record group ideas on this sheet.)

Encourager:_____
(Ensure that all students participate, support the criticism of ideas not people, and suggest the direction for the group's work.)

Major concepts(s) we would emphasize from "I Have A Dream."
1.

2.

Problematic Situation of paper group created (use back of paper if necessary)

Luther King, Jr. (1968). A problematic situation is a prereading strategy in which teachers create problems for students to solve as a way of directing their schema to promote reading comprehension. I randomly assigned the students to groups of three (university students do not always need to be placed in predetermined groups). Then, I asked that they sit facing each other at their tables. The students in each group were assigned one of the following roles: timer, recorder, or encourager. These responsibilities were described on the project handout. I briefly outlined the project to the students, and they went to work. As students worked on this project, I walked among them, listening and observing and answering questions.

Semantic Webbing

Another cooperative group activity that I use in my reading methods course is semantic webbing (see Bromley, 1991). One way that I use it in my teaching is to model how teachers can use webs with children. Webs can also be used with college reading assignments.

First, I place the preservice teachers in groups of four at their tables. Next, I write a topic on the board and ask them to brainstorm that topic with the other students at their table. Students quickly generate a list of words that are related to the topic (see Figure 8.2). For example, I modeled how to use a *Ranger Rick* article by Robson (1989) called "The Z Team," about jobs at the zoo. I asked the students to brainstorm probable kinds of jobs one could have in a zoo. Students brainstormed this topic in groups of four at their tables. After they brainstormed for 3-4 minutes, I recorded their responses on the board:

> vet
> feeder
> ticket-taker/cashier
> cage cleaners
> administrator
> fund-raisers
> vendor for animal treats
> animal trainer
> demonstrator/educator for zoo customers about animals
> gift store clerk
> janitors

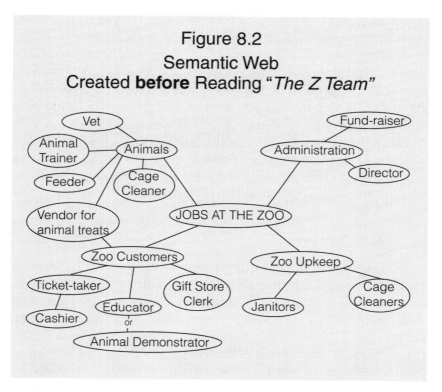

Figure 8.2

Semantic Web

Created before Reading "The Z Team"

Next, I asked the students to develop various categories for these named jobs. The students discussed possible categories at their tables and then I listed one job from each group on the board in semantic webbing map form (see Figure 8.3).

Then students placed the jobs under the appropriate categories. Sometimes this was done as a whole group, using the map on the board, and other times it was done with one map for each group at their table.

How the rest of this strategy is implemented varies, depending on the text materials that are read by the students. If the text is difficult, then the students might write a brief essay about the topic using the map as a guide. When the material is easier to read, I direct them to the text. Following the reading I ask them to add what they have learned from the reading to their maps. Either way, the maps help surface the prior knowledge and offer a visual framework, both of which serve to increase student comprehension. (Figure 8.4 outlines these steps.)

Figure 8.3
Semantic Web
Created **after** Reading *"The Z Team"*

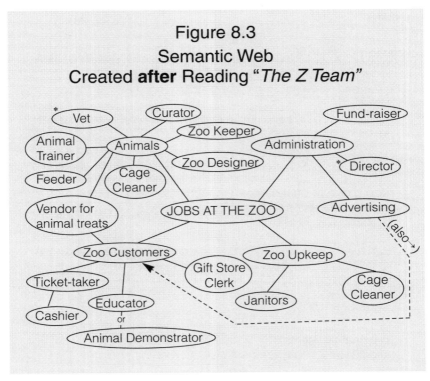

Overall, when I use Cooperative Learning strategies, I use real issues that are meaningful to preservice teachers. I believe that it is especially important for the students to learn how to work with each other, not only because it strengthens the community of the classroom, but because it also prepares the students for cooperative team situations that they will encounter in the teaching profession. Teachers participate collectively in their schools on textbook adoption committees, grade-level meetings, department meetings, discipline hearing committees, and through in-service activities. More and more administrators are seeking input from teachers about school decisions. Through using Cooperative Learning strategies, preservice teachers can be prepared to work together to meet the challenges of society.

Figure 8.4
EE 312: Prereading Activity—Semantic Webbing

The prereading semantic mapping activity proceeds as follows:

1. The teacher writes on the chalkboard the topic that the students are going to read about.

2. The teacher asks student groups to brainstorm all the ideas they can think of related to the topic. The teacher lists one idea from each group on the board. After each group lists an idea, the teacher asks students to add other ideas that are not listed on the board.

3. Students label each category. The teacher assists by helping them focus on what the words have in common.

4. Students use the categories to create a map. This may be done in the small groups.

5. (Optional) Students write a brief composition, using the map as a guide, in which they tell what they know about the topic.

6. Students then read the passage to learn more about the topic.

7. After reading the selection, students are asked to add new ideas acquired from the reading to each category of the map. This helps them link new concepts with their prior knowledge.

What are ways that semantic mapping facilitates comprehension?

REFERENCES

Bromley, K. D. (1991). Webbing with Literature. Boston: Allyn and Bacon.

King, Jr., M. L. (1968). I have a dream. The annals of America. (1961-1968: The Burdens of World Power), volume 18, pp. 156-59. Chicago: Encyclopedia Britannica.

Robson, A. (1989). The Z Team. *Ranger Rick* 23(5): 23-25.

9

ACTIVE LEARNING IN HISTORY CLASSES

by Peter Frederick

> Tell me, and I'll listen
> Show me, and I'll understand
> Involve me, and I'll learn.
> Lakota Indian

I believe that the great challenge confronting historians today is the challenge of the classroom. To meet it we shall have to give to teaching a higher place in our scale of values than we do today . . . We shall ourselves have to be the best teachers that we know how to be, the most humane, the most sympathetic, the most dedicated.

> —Deter Perkins, American Historical Association (AHA) presidential address, December 1956

and thirty years later . . .

I am suggesting that unless we restore to the teaching of history at every level that humanistic aspect that sees history primarily as the story of people living in a distant time and in another place—unless we do that we lose the greatest strength that history has to offer . . . Teaching history well is one of the best things a person can do.

> —Gerda Lerner, Organization of American Historians (OAH) address to teachers, April 1986

This work is adapted and reprinted by permission of *Teaching History*, Emporia State University, Emporia, KS 66801 and is cited as follows: Peter Frederick. (Fall, 1991). Active learning in history classes. *Teaching History: A Journal of Methods* 16(2): 67-83.

Henry Adams had a problem. Actually, he had several, not least his incomplete education as he pursued thirteenth-century unity in the midst of twentieth-century multiplicity. Adams, moreover, was concerned with the moral collapse of American politics, which mirrored the decline of the Adams family itself.

Descended from two former presidents and a distinguished diplomat father, Henry was "just" an historian. But the immediate problem he faced in 1870, as Charles Eliot called him to teach medieval history at Harvard, was how to do it.

Adams began his academic career in a way familiar to thousands of subsequent history professors: No one helped him learn how to teach. Worse yet, he did not know much about his field. Adams confessed later in *The Education of Henry Adams* (Adams, 1918) that he had not given more than "an hour, more or less, to the Middle Ages," knowing only "enough to be ignorant." Although contemporary historians, unlike Adams, "know their field," many have little if any preparation in how to teach it. The highest challenge we face is to motivate our students to love history as we do by involving them more actively in its study.

Henry Adams tried several approaches to involve his students in class: discussions, lectures, and seminars. He decided that he wanted to get students "to talk," which meant "he had to devise schemes to find what they were thinking about, and induce them to risk criticism from their fellows." But Adams could not discover what was on his students' mind, he reported, in part because "their professor had nothing in his." Discouraged with discussions, Adams shifted to lectures, which he thought appropriate to a course on the twelfth century. But lecturing did not suit Adams at all, he wrote, because he wanted "to teach his students something not wholly useless." Only one in ten, he estimated, was stimulated by what he had to say.

Finally Adams resolved to "cultivate this tenth mind" by involving students in a seminar to instruct them in the use of the "historical method" as a way of finding out what he and they did not know. After a period of illusory pleasure with this system, Adams concluded that "his wonderful method led nowhere" and was "doomed to failure." He declared both himself and the educational system "fallacious". After six years he was content neither with what he had taught nor with the way he had taught it, and resigned. He had "tried a great many experiments, and wholly succeeded in none." [1]

History professors today, unlike Adams, do not have the luxury of an independent income and therefore must teach. And we do so "gladly," as Perkins (1956) said in his AHA presidential address. Nevertheless, like Henry Adams we, too, struggle with the challenge of getting students motivated and involved with the texts, themes, issues, and questions of history that excite us. Many of us have tried in vain to get students to talk. Many, too, have encountered classes of students who confessed that they thought history was "boring," "a bunch of names and dates and facts." Although there are small signs of recent resurgence, history enrollments have declined in the past two decades. Cultural priorities partly explain the flight.

But the discipline of history suffers from internal fragmentation as well as from external social attitudes. As one representative historian complained in an OAH survey, history has become "excessively compartmentalized and irrelevant except to our own diminishing numbers." David Thelen (1986), who reported on the survey, expressed his surprise not that there was a gap between narrow scholarship and the "generalist" goals and needs of most historians, but rather with "the depth and breadth of dissatisfaction with 'overspecialization' of scholarship."

"Our academic arrogance," Weisberger (1987) wrote, has "allowed many professors to lose touch with their base in popular culture." The irony he points out, is that just as the study of history has expanded to include more and more social groups and public purposes, historians have widened the gap between themselves and others—including students. Although "history is not sick," Weisberger writes, "the teaching of history may be."[1] Some critics, such as Theodore Hamerow, Gertrude Himmelfarb, and Bernard Bailyn, blame the new social history for the loss of a coherent narrative story of the past. Many others, such as Thomas Bender, Robert Kelley, and

Carl Degler, call for incorporating social history into a new narrative synthesis. Multiculturalism adds to the challenge.

In the *OAH Newsletter*, McGregor and McGregor (1988) summarized many current dissatisfactions: "We stand justly accused," they wrote, "of writing only for one another." But unlike other critics, they took action by conducting a summer institute for secondary history teachers on the new social history and in developing pedagogical materials to help students learn it. Their experience was not entirely a happy one. They concluded that "the chasm between history taught at the secondary level and history researched at the university level seems very wide and imposing." But surely, a similar gap exists in post-secondary history teaching as well.

These colleagues exhort us, as did Perkins (1956) and Lerner (1986), thirty years apart, to devote more energy and creativity to bridging the chasm between scholarly specialization and our responsibilities to both the public and our students to teach history well. As Hoff-Wilson (1986) wrote, a recurring theme in her annual reports to OAH on the various crises besetting the historical profession, the crisis "involving better teaching of history in secondary and higher educational institutions (especially the survey classes) remains very much with us."

This article seeks to support the need to achieve "better teaching of history" by suggesting several practical strategies for involving students more actively in the history classroom, thus revitalizing their and our enthusiasm for learning history in colleges and universities. Nowhere is this challenge more important than in survey courses. The suggestions made here, though applicable to history courses at any level, are focused on building active learning into the survey classes. These strategies are appropriate for any size class—40 or 400—and for any kind of room, even a conventionally tiered lecture hall with students in chairs bolted to the floor in rows facing a lone professor standing behind a lectern.

Every study of effective educational practices[2] in recent years, including studies in medical education, cites active and small-group cooperative learning, high expectations, and the giving of caring, constructive, and frequent feedback to students, as the most crucial elements for learning. Despite the consistency of these recommendations, most college and university professors, historians among them, in most classes most of the time, continue to lecture to passive and increasingly inattentive, unmotivated audiences. We lecture for many compelling reasons, as we have all said: "I'd like to do less lecturing, but there's too much to cover." Or, "I teach the survey and I've got to get from the fall of Rome to the French Revolution. Or, "I'd like to try some new methods, but I can't—I have 300 students in the class, you know." Or, "Student interaction is impossible in my classroom—the chairs are in rows bolted to the floor—all I can do is lecture." Or, "With all the recent criticisms of how little college students know about American history and geography, I'd better lecture to make sure they know the important facts."

There are valid reasons for lecturing, and it is not my intention to repudiate the use of lectures to achieve such legitimate learning goals. It is wrong to assume that students listening to a lecture are necessarily inactive. Lectures are necessary to impart new information and to structure an important topic or series of events, or to explain, clarify, and organize difficult concepts, or to analyze and compare relationships among two cultures or two different eras, or to tell a compellingly interesting story, such as the course and significance of the defeat of the Spanish Armada, or the Seneca Falls convention, or the election of 1912. Lectures, most importantly, can inspire student enthusiasm for further learning and informed right actions, in Emerson's words, "to set the hearts of youth on flame."

Unfortunately, not all lectures meet the Emersonian standard. Even when they do, there is substantial evidence of diminishing attention and retention after about 20 minutes. The point, however, is not to quit lecturing but rather to vary our lectures with active learning strategies. The lecture is but one instructional method among many, all intended to increase ways of involving students actively in large impersonal history classes. Our choice of strategy depends on our goals. When "covering" or synthesizing new material, no doubt we can lecture. But for teaching students to decipher documents, to detect historical interpretations and develop their own, to distinguish underlying and proximate causes of events, and to appreciate the complexity of human motivation, much less to learn how to write and speak well, students need to be more active learners.

Three pervasive principles are important for active learning. The first principle is that, given the fact that students have diverse learning styles, teachers should use a variety of different teaching strategies. We need to vary our methods not only on different days but also within any single class period. To continually reenergize students, recapture their attention, and aid their learning, we need to have energy shifts about every 20 minutes, in which both the activity and the voices that speak are changed. For example, after listening to 15-20 minutes of a lecture on how Puritan theology gave energy to Massachusetts Bay, students will need a few minutes to absorb and integrate what they have learned. They need to reflect, ask questions, and repeat their understanding of covenant theology, or how one knows one is saved (no easy task). After hearing several students struggle to explain, in Edmund Morgan's (1958) terms, how one seeks to purify a flawed institution by leaving it, students may need the teacher's clarification. Within a 50-minute period, the energy shifts twice as students listen to a concept explained, work with it themselves, and then get feedback on their understanding of the concept.

The second crucial pervasive principle for learning is that students need visual reinforcements. Like it or not, we compete not just with TV but with MTV. The larger the class the more need for the visual support of chalkboards, handouts, and overhead transparencies. In our class on Puritanism it would help to have the essential points of Calvinism and of Winthrop's "city on a hill" speech on the *Arabella* listed somewhere, as well as to see on a map the geographical relationship between Old and New England. Personalizing an issue is also a way of visualizing it. Pick a student, John, for example, in the third row, who like a good Puritan is concerned with the question of whether or not he is saved and how knowing that might make a difference in the kind of life he leads. Focusing on John is a way of activating the involvement of the entire class and making abstract issues concrete and personal.

Or consider the evocative power of slides, not just in a slide-lecture, but as a way of involving every student actively in the interpretation of a single visual image. For example, show a slide (or overhead transparency) of a Thomas Nast or Herblock cartoon, or a photograph of a family or famous scene (Pearl Harbor or Kent State), or a presidential campaign poster, or a powerful painting or lithograph of an historical scene. Ask students first to describe what they see and then to analyze what it means, perhaps even to suggest a title or caption. My favorite is painter John Gast's "Westward-Ho," also known as "American Progress," which shows Indians, buffalo, and a bear fleeing westward as Miss Liberty, carrying a schoolbook and stringing telegraph wire, brings light and "civilization" as she leads miners, farmers, ranchers, stage coaches, wagon trains, and railroads across the country. There are lots of details to describe. The analysis includes noting the various stages of westward "development" as well as a debate on whether to title the painting from the perspective of the settlers from the east or those fleeing off the edge to the west.

The third pervasive principle is that students will retain their learning when they are able to claim ownership of it. This will happen more often to the extent that we can hook their experiences to our teaching goals, which is partly achieved by the examples we choose. If we provide spaces, or holes, in the content we are presenting, students will fill in the spaces with their own insights, reading, analysis, or experience.

The Puritan dilemma, for example, which is usually discussed early in a U.S. survey class when students are still adjusting to their housing assignment, is more easily comprehended when they are invited to connect their understanding of the dilemma to their own situation, in this case living with others in a dorm or sorority or fraternity house. Assuming students have some ideal of social relationships, how do they handle the imperfections of their current living arrangement, and what options do they have in trying to achieve better human interactions, in an imperfect situation? As they explore various options, they might begin to understand John

Winthrop's dilemma of whether or not to leave the Church of England in seeking to purify it.

These three principles of learning—diverse methods and energy shifts, visual reinforcements, and ownership—permeate the active learning strategies described in this article. The strategies, or teaching ideas, are grouped into six sections: interactive lectures; questioning; using small groups in large classes; critical-thinking and problem-solving exercises; large class debates and role-playing; and affective learning through the use of media.

1. INTERACTIVE LECTURES

The interactive lecture involves various forms of student participation in the process of ordering a topic into a coherent pattern. In one form, you invite students to help create a lecture by brainstorming. When beginning a new topic, start by asking students to call out "everything you know or think you know about World War I" (or Darwinism, China, slavery, the Renaissance, the Constitutional Convention, or whatever). As you record ideas on an overhead transparency or blackboard, a list will unfold of a mixture of specific names, dates, and events; descriptions of natural phenomena and human experience; feelings and prejudices; and possibly even interpretive judgments. Students bring to most courses both a degree of familiarity and considerable misinformation. Brainstorming provides teachers with a quick sense of the class, including its interpretive point of view. To ask students to call out what they know about slavery, for example, as an introduction to that topic elicits many images about the politics of the Civil War and the physical horrors of slavery but very little about slave culture and community. Another use of brainstorming is to invite students to suggest everything that comes to mind in defining a key term: *romanticism*, for example, or *progressivism*, or *imperialism*, or *feminism*.

Since "anything goes," brainstorming provides an opportunity for many students to participate as well as for faculty to find out what students already know and don't know. The only rule of brainstorming is to acknowledge every comment by writing it down, thus both providing visual reinforcements and honoring the student contributions. As ideas are proposed, clever teachers might arrange the ideas in rough groupings, perhaps political, economic, social, and cultural. Alternatively, one might ask students to suggest appropriate categories and to comment on the accuracy and relative importance of the array of events, experiences, and interpretations. Refinements can be dealt with by erasures, a luxury not allowed in the formal lecture. Thus begins the jointly created coherent understanding of the topic.

In an interactive, participatory lecture it is necessary, as in any lecture, for the professor to have a clear idea of what should be revealed and discovered in the process. Some key points about slavery, or World War I, or feminism, surely must be made. At the same time, however, it is imperative that teachers guard against excessive manipulation and be free and flexible enough to depart from their preconceived ideas. The final creation should legitimately reflect both student and teacher conceptions of what is important about a topic. When the class is over, the teacher and students will have created an organized configuration of salient points and concepts. In this interactive process, students spend more time thinking than recording as they concentrate on contributing to the evolving "lecture" before them.

Obviously, the participatory lecture can be done badly. When students have not brought to the class the knowledge provided by their prior experience or reading, or when the professor manipulates student statements to a rigidly preconceived schema, the experience can be dreary. But when the mutual participation is free and open, students are actively engaged and teachers might even learn new insights about how to view historical material. Although obviously less efficient than a traditional lecture, the participatory lecture involves many students actively and can be done in any size auditorium.

A variation of the interactive lecture is to ask students at the beginning of class to call out one concrete visual image that stands out from a particular reading, event, cultural object, or period of time. "From your reading about the

Constitutional Convention (or Frederick Douglass's life, or the Pullman Strike, or Mary Fish's experiences in the American Revolution, or the 1920s, etc.), what one specific scene, event, or moment stands out in your mind?" The recall of concrete scenes prompts further recollections, and a flood of images flows from the students. As students report their images, list them on an overhead transparency or blackboard, thus providing a visual backdrop to the lecture or discussion that follows. After a few minutes, ask the class: What themes seem to emerge from these items?" "What connects these images?" "Is there a pattern to our recollected events?" "What is missing?"

In this inductive approach, facts precede analysis, the learning moves from lower order "what happened" questions to higher order "why" and "what do you think and feel about it?" questions. A few minutes hearing concrete descriptive images at the beginning of a traditional lecture (or in the middle) activates student energy, enhances the vividness of the content for the day, and helps students visualize the professor's analysis of the meaning of that content. Moreover, many students get to say something early in class and every contribution gets written down to aid the collective memory and provide a visual backdrop and reinforcement to learning.

Another way to introduce a new topic—or to check on learning halfway through one—is to ask students to make statements they think are true about some particular issue. "It is true about the Vietnam War that . . . " "We have agreed that it is true about the New Deal. . . " "It is true about Reconstruction that . . . " And so on. I have found this strategy useful for dealing with a topic—slavery or the American Indians, for example—where demythologizing may be necessary. This exercise reveals the complexity and ambiguity of knowledge as students present their truth statements and other students raise questions about or refute them. It also generates a list of questions and issues demanding further study.

2. USING QUESTIONS FOR INVOLVEMENT

The generation and appropriate use of questions is at the heart of learning and is an obvious way to shift energy back and forth in large classes. Teachers ask rhetorical questions all the time in lectures. But we can also ask real ones, and expect responses. There are several approaches.

From the movie *The Paper Chase* we all have an indelibly stereotyped view of one method of asking questions in large classes. One student is singled out and interrogated unmercifully in order to tease out the significance of a particular legal case. When I watch actor John Houseman at work, I always think of Socrates, who was a mixture of a great teacher genuinely guiding others to their own self-discoveries and a skillfully manipulative intellectual hustler steering others to his desired answers. We teachers, too, can do variations of the same approach, presumably more mercifully than either Houseman or Socrates.

One approach is to address a somewhat open-ended question to the class: "What were the causes of the Civil War? Or, "What major constitutional questions have persisted throughout American history?" Or, "What is the meaning of the green light at the end of Daisy's dock?" Or, What was the Renaissance?" Or even, "Why was Socrates condemned to death?" A student answer is met with a follow-up question directed at the class generally. We need not put one person on the spot, for the primary point is to convey substantive content and raise further questions through a participatory question and answer format. In the end, as in brainstorming, a number of points and arguments are articulated, and probably should be listed on the board. A further question can invite students to begin to analyze critically the various arguments: "Which of these points, or arguments, or definitions makes the most sense to you, and why?"

A second approach to questioning, perhaps the next step, is to put a question to the class and ask three students sitting next to one another to explore it for five minutes. "How would you, as a nineteenth-century married woman, assert your autonomy?" "Do you think Truman had the authority to send troops into Korea?" "Would you have voted for Socrates' death? Why or why not?" The best kinds of questions are not those simply seeking information but those requiring students to make judgments and choices among compelling alternatives. After only five minutes in the trios, enormous energy can be generated by putting questions to the class: "How would you assert your autonomy?" Or, "How many would have voted to put Socrates to death?" "How many not?" "Why?" A lecture could indeed have presented both the pertinent information and alternatives more efficiently but without the interaction, dispersal of energy, and multiplicity of voices, points of view, and controversy. The students own more of their learning.

So far we have looked at questions we ask. But students have their own questions, and even in large classes we can provide ways for them to ask those questions and learn how to formulate better ones. Being able to ask questions about a particular text or issue is essential in coming to terms with it. There are many ways of generating student questions. Ask students to prepare ahead of time (on Wednesday for Friday's class) one or two questions about their reading or a topic and bring them to class. One way to put the assignment to them is as follows: "A question I still have about the immigrant experience (or Puritanism, the New Deal, the sexuality of slavery, or whatever) but have been afraid to ask, is . . ." Students can either walk into Friday's class with their questions or be invited to put them on cards and submit them ahead of time, a technique that helps reticent students present their questions.

Another variation is to ask students as they enter the classroom to call out questions about the text or topic they hope will be answered that day. At the end of the hour ask them to write down one or two still unresolved questions they want explored at the next class (as well as the one or two most significant things they learned that day). Or, at some point halfway through a period, divide the class into pairs or small groups of three or four and ask them to "take five minutes and agree on one question that you think is crucial to explore further." This will sort out fewer, more thoughtful questions. In addition, and importantly, this task leads to some peer teaching and learning as one member of a group answers another's query in the course of the search for consensus on a question. Hearing student questions is an excellent way, in addition to brief, one-minute written reports, for a professor to get feedback on how well students are learning. The quality and substance of their questions indicates both areas of strength and gaps in understanding.

A "press conference" questioning variation is a good way to conclude a unit. Students are invited, as investigative reporters, to ask questions of their teacher about the topic they have been studying. They may seek to clarify confusing material, or to find out new information or, like a budding Socrates or Mike Wallace, to press their professor's interpretation of an issue to a point of contradiction or inadequate evidence. The teacher's responses might be crisp and short, or could constitute minilectures. Professors can structure questioning sessions in any number of imaginative ways to facilitate and humanize the learning process. In any event, this lecture hall variation is feasible in any size class, provides interaction, energy shifts, and different voices, and underlines the importance of students' responsibility for their own learning.

3. SMALL GROUPS IN LARGE CLASSES

The strategies mentioned thus far suggest that active learning is enhanced by breaking large classes into small groups. No matter the size of a class, it can always be broken down into groups of two, five, eight, or whatever, thus serving many purposes. The first is to provide energy shifts and interaction, enabling more students to think during class, to write or say something, and to generate more ideas about a text or topic. Groups also lend themselves to a healthy, competitive spirit, whether asked to or not, as students in one group are inevitably interested in "what they're doing over there." Moreover, there is potentially more intimacy in the class when it is broken into groups. Not only do students get to know each other, but also the teacher has an opportunity to establish personal contact with more students as he or she moves around listening to the small-group discussions. Furthermore, reticent students find it easier to express themselves in the smaller groups and can gain some confidence in speaking up, which is not possible in the larger setting.

There are three crucial points to consider in helping small groups to work and learn efficiently. First, the instructions should be clear, simple, and task-oriented. Examples: "What do you think is the crucial turning point in Malcolm X's life?" "Which person in *The Iliad* best represents the qualities of a Greek hero?" "Which example of imperialism defines it best, and why?" "What options did slaves have to seek their freedom or assert their self-worth? "Look at the map and explain Iran's strategic importance to both the United States and the Soviet Union." "Identify three positive and three negative features of Lyndon Johnson's administration." "Generate a list of restrictions on women's freedom in the 1850s." "If you were Lincoln, what would you do about Fort Sumter?"

Second, the groups should be given a sense of how much time they have to do their work. "Take ten minutes to define your group's position or decision." And third, be sure to ask each group to select a recorder and to provide ways of reporting back and debriefing the process. In smaller classes one way is to invite each group briefly to state their conclusion(s) orally in turn, with the teacher recording them on the board. Another is to ask the recorder from each group to write its conclusions on a transparency or on newsprint posted around the room. Still another is to ask the groups to write their ideas down, to be collected, collated, and reported by the professor at the next class. Yet another strategy is to ask students first to write for a couple of minutes on the question before getting into groups. Both the writing and the group discussion provide space for the student to explore, or "own," his or her thoughts before the general discussion.

In very large lecture classes with 200-400 students, writing and breaking up into pairs or trios will provide that space. At an appropriate point, interrupt your lecture to ask two or three students sitting next to each other to discuss an issue or question together for a few minutes, perhaps preceded by writing. "What's the most important point I've been making for the past ten minutes?" "Which explanation of the causes of the Civil War makes the most sense to you?" "Who is the real hero here?" "What's the major constitutional concern in this case?" "Which aspect of Puritan theology bothers you the most and why?" After as little as three or four minutes, invite volunteers to call out their conclusions and concerns. Obviously, one needs only to hear a sampling of the trios to get a sense of the level of understanding of the class.

This process provides public affirmation of the thinking of a roomful of students, thus giving feedback both to other students and to the teacher on how well they understand a particular topic. Even "wrong" feedback is instructive and can dictate the next appropriate minilecture and reading assignment. Without this brief energy shift into small groups the professor might not have known the gaps in student knowledge and gone ahead into the next unit, at the cost of losing a good portion of the class. Moreover, the break not only gives students an opportunity to hear a variety of other voices but also reenergizes them (wakes them up, perhaps), making it more likely they will listen more attentively to the teacher's next 20 minutes of lecturing.

4. CRITICAL THINKING AND PROBLEM SOLVING

These suggestions have been predicated upon shifts of energy and voice in about 20-minute blocks of teaching time, thus supporting the conventional wisdom about student attention. A typical 50-minute class period, therefore, should usually involve three segments in various orders: a mini lecture, a small-group active student experience, and some general interaction and feedback. Other activities are perhaps even more appropriate to this alternating approach, especially in helping students develop critical thinking and problem-solving skills.

The problem-solving lecture begins with a question, or an enigma, or a compellingly unfinished human story that ends with an unresolved problem that hooks student interest. "What will happen to the confident Athenians in Sicily?" "What brought Captain Parker's men to Lexington Green that cold April morning?" "Why did the handsome Crown Prince Rudolf, heir to the throne of the Austro-Hungarian Empire, kill Mary Vetsera and himself?" "What will Lincoln do?" "Will the freedmen on the Allston plantations achieve their goals in those chaotic months of 1865?" "What will happen to this young immigrant woman as she arrives in New York?" As these examples suggest, it is best to tell a story that focuses clearly on a human decision or fate. The answer, no doubt a complex one involving historical narrative, unfolds during the class hour; if skillfully developed, the unfolding will be completed with only a few minutes left in the period.

Resolving historical human dilemmas is an effective way to break a class period into alternating chunks of time and dispersed energy. The problem, or question, is woven throughout the lecture, inviting students to fill in spaces in the story with their own unfolding outcomes as they listen. Or, to break the narrative after 15-20 minutes, the resolution could be an interactive process in which the teacher elicits the students' proposed completions of a story, lists them on the board or an overhead, and discusses them. "What do you think will happen?" "Which outcome to this story makes the most sense to you?" If there is no consensus, the teacher lectures a little more, invites a new set of student responses and asks the question again. Ideally, when the narrative is finally resolved, most students will have figured it out for themselves as the class ends.

The most important skill our students need is how to read, and the large-class lecture setting also provides an opportunity to practice an old-fashioned but woefully ignored technique: *explication du texte*. We can teach our students how to read, even in large lecture classes, by going directly to a text and reading and analyzing passages together out loud. At first, the professor models how to read and interpret a passage. The students, following along in their books (or on handouts or an overhead projection), observe the professor working through a selection from a speech, sermon, essay, poem, or fictional passage. In the survey courses one can also spend important class time early in the term showing how to read and highlight a survey textbook.

Then it is their turn: how better for students to develop their reading skills, and to think like historians, than to see close textual analysis modeled, followed by an opportunity to practice analyzing a text themselves. There are many ways to select appropriate passages and structure such a class. Invite students, either ahead of time (preferably) or at the start of class, to "find one or two quotations from the text you find particularly significant." Or, "Find one quotation you especially liked and one you disliked." Or, "Identify a passage that you think best illustrates the major thesis of the chapter."

Students are then ready to read these passages out loud and discuss them. "Jennifer, would you please read the top paragraph on page 144?" Be sure to pause long enough for everyone to find the right spot in their book: "Top of page 144—is everyone with us?" Lively and illuminating engagement is guaranteed because not all students select the same quotations nor do they all interpret passages the same way. With a particularly ambiguous passage, small groups of three or four students could be asked to struggle with the meaning. "Three of you sitting next to each other: Put your heads together and in your own words state what you think is the main point of the passage: What's it mean?" Or, "What's happening here?" Invite a few groups to report their reflections, giving the teacher an opportunity to react to the substance of their interpretation, comparing it to his or her own thoughts. Breaking into small groups disperses the energy and provides practice and feedback for students before they return to the professor's voice and analysis. After having struggled with a passage themselves for a few minutes, students will gain more from hearing the teacher's interpretation.

This process of modeling how to read analytically can be done for other than just verbal texts. Art historians, musicologists, economists, and anthropologists have traditionally used lectures to demonstrate how to "read" an abstract painting, or sonata allegro form, or a supply and demand curve, or artifact. Historians can use the lecture period for "history labs" to train students in other critical skills: how to do quantitative analysis of graphs, charts, and tables; how to interpret census data; and how to read maps. Many of us hand out short historical documents in class—a tax record, a household inventory, a diary entry, a folktale, a will, a ship's manifest, an old tool, a family photograph—and ask: "What do you see? What does the document say?" After teasing as much descriptive content out of a document, then ask the higher-order questions of significance: "What does it mean? What implications can you draw from the document on how people lived?" To summarize: make sure students have a copy of the source in question in front of them (or visual access through slides and overhead transparencies), and then follow three steps: model how to interpret the document, have the students practice, and provide feedback.

5. LARGE-CLASS DEBATES AND ROLE-PLAYING

Although assigning specific tasks to small groups of students disperses the energy in large classes, not all instructors are comfortable with the uncertainty and potential lack of control implicit in the decentralized large class. Let me suggest, therefore, some ways of achieving more student participation and engagement in large history classes without changing the professor's central controlling role in the classroom.

The debate, formal or otherwise, is an energizing way of involving students actively in the classroom. Although neither one of two polar sides of an issue obviously contains the whole truth, it is pedagogically desirable to force students to choose one or the other side of a dichotomous question and to defend their choice. Consider, even in a large lecture setting, a debate on such questions as the following "Was Burke or Paine more right about the French Revolution?" "Was Nat Turner's revolt justified?" "If you are a black sharecropper in 1905, does Booker T. Washington or W. E. B. Du Bois have the better strategy for your progress?" "Should the United States annex the Philippines or not in 1898?" "The United States: Melting Pot or Preserver of Cultural Identity?" "Vietnam: Hawks or Doves?" Some of the old Amherst series (Taylor, 1950s-1960s) problems in American civilization might still make excellent debates: "John D. Rockefeller—Robber Baron or Industrial Statesman?" Or "The New Deal—Revolution or Evolution?"

The logistics are not as difficult as one might imagine. One obvious strategy is to take advantage of the central aisle, dividing large lecture halls in order to structure debates. Students can either support the side of an issue assigned to the half of the hall where they happen to be sitting. Or, as prearranged in conjunction with the stimulation of a film or reading assignment, they could come to class prepared to take a seat on one side or another. When I have taught in a large auditorium with two doors, I have put up signs over the doors directing students to the two sides: "Burke" and "Paine." Once students have physically, as it were, put their bodies on the line, they are more receptive to answering a simple question: "Why have you chosen to sit where you are?" That is usually enough to spark a rather lively debate.

In a large class, more structure is necessary. The following process permits the professor to maintain rigorous control from the podium in leading the debate: "From the right side of the hall we will hear five statements on behalf of the 'Hawk' side of U.S. involvement in Vietnam (or Burke's position), after which we will hear five statements from the left on behalf of the 'Dove' side (or Paine's position)." The process can be repeated, including rebuttals, before concluding by asking for two or three volunteers to make summary arguments for each side, and perhaps a final vote. Sometimes though the class ends, the argument continues all day long.

Most important questions, however, do not divide into halves. Our good students would never settle for forced dichotomous choices. When some students (quite rightly) refuse to choose one side or the other, create a middle ground and space and invite their reasons for choosing it. Some large lecture halls have two central aisles, which makes legitimizing a third position both intellectually defensible and logistically possible. "Those who repudiate both the Hawks and the Doves (or Burke and Paine) for what you think is a more reasonable position, sit in the middle." Now three groups are invited to state their positions. The dimensions of learning increase. Students in the middle, for example, might learn how difficult it is to try to remain neutral on heated emotional issues during revolutionary times.

Role-playing is another strategy with powerful potential for learning by injecting energy, emotions, and interactions in a large classroom. One form is for the professor to enter the class in the role of historical figure (including dress and props) to give a speech or sermon and invite questions. Another is to give several students (or groups) time to research several historical characters and bring them together on stage for some variation of a panel, press conference, debate, or dinner party. The figures are usually well-known people: Benjamin Franklin, Sojourner Truth, Horace Mann, Teddy Roosevelt, Emma Goldman, or Malcolm X. The intellectual convictions, controversies, and contradictions of real people are brought out by this kind of role-playing.

But the strategy can also be used to illuminate the experiences and difficult choices of anonymous ordinary people in social groups. There are many simulation games on contemporary issues and social conflict in history and the social sciences, but most are too expensive, complex, and time-consuming to use in our large classes. Therefore, one can create less elaborate situations in which historical groups struggle with conflicting interests and roles.

The process is not as complicated as one might think. First, a minilecture establishes the context and setting for the role-playing. Second, the class is divided into a number of small groups (of varying sizes and including collective roles depending on class size), each group assigned a clearly delineated role, usually of a group. Third, each group is given a specific, concrete task—usually to propose a position and course of action. And fourth, the proposals emanating from different groups will inevitably conflict with each other in some way—racially, regionally, ideologically, tactically, or over scarce funds, land, jobs, power, or resources. Given these conflicts, closure is as difficult to achieve in a role-play as in history itself.

The following examples will suggest others. One of my favorites is to set up a New England town meeting in 1779, in which a variety of groups (landed elite, yeoman farmers, Tory loyalists, militiamen and soldiers of the Continental army, lawyers, ministers, and tradesmen, etc.) are charged with drafting instructions for delegates to a state constitutional convention. Another is to challenge several groups in the summer of 1865—defeated Confederates, southern Unionists, victorious northern Republicans, moderate northerners, and the freedmen—to develop lists of their goals and the strategies for accomplishing them. Still another is to put a whole class (working in small groups) into the same situation, say, emancipated slaves on a Texas plantation in 1865, or unskilled and skilled immigrant steelworkers facing a lockout in Pennsylvania in 1892, or female abolitionists in the 1830s, or civil rights activists in the 1960s, and ask them to decide in each case what to do to enhance their freedom. A political history variation is to make yourself a national leader facing a serious crisis, say, Napoleon in 1799, or Lincoln in 1861, or FDR in 1933, and create "brain trust" groups on different issues to advise you.

Given careful planning, clear directions, assertive leadership, and a lot of luck, the format of group role-playing can fulfill many objectives. One could hear the proposals of different groups and immediately incorporate them into a lecture on how what really happened reflected many of these same conflicts. Or, one could carry out the role-playing process longer by structuring a meeting or convention to consider the differing groups' proposals. The student groups could be instructed to prepare speeches; to caucus to develop strategies, coalitions, and tactics for achieving their goals; and to see the deliberations through to some conclusion. Neat, simple, clear closures are not easy (short of the class-ending buzzer), but this variation for large lecture classes has tremendous potential for experiential learning, and of course involves enormous energy and interaction.

In all these role-playing situations the professor should play an active role, as moderator of the meetings or as the President, organizing and carefully monitoring the interactions. Because role-playing in conflicting groups can get heated, emotional, and potentially out of control, it is necessary to wield a vigorous gavel and forcefully direct the process. This in itself models another point about leadership in history. Whenever teachers wish to restore order they can terminate the role-playing and shift to debriefing what was learned from the experience about the realities of the historical experience. This is, of course, crucial, and a rule of thumb of role-playing is to spend as much time debriefing in order to clarify what was learned as in doing the exercise in the first place. After debriefing, the professor makes the transition to the next topic and pedagogical approach, which, after role-playing, would probably be a synthetic summary lecture.

6. AFFECTIVE LEARNING WITH AUDIOVISUAL MEDIA

No account of engaging students in the active learning of history is complete without acknowledging the power of media for inspiring student motivation. Much has been written on the use of films and other audiovisual techniques. This section will focus on the role of slides and music in evoking students' emotional learning. This is a seriously neglected but crucial area of teaching and learning, for we need to teach to both sides of students' brains. Emotion has surely played an enormous role in history, therefore, it belongs in the classroom, not just because the use of media "hooks" the student and is motivating but also because evoking emotions can set the tone of a topic, raise questions, deepen analysis, and compel review and rethinking. In short, emotional experience leads to cognitive insights.

Here are some examples. As students enter the classroom, it is an opportune time to establish a mood to ready them for the content for a particular class period. At the beginning of class, show some slides, say, of war scenes, or of farm life in the Great Plains, or of men and women performing gender-distinct roles, or of material culture objects. Or, as they walk in, play a recording of an inspiring speech—FDR, or Churchill or Malcolm X. Or, have music playing, say, Civil War, labor movement, or civil rights songs. Or, put several powerful short quotations on a transparency or place several objects around the lecture hall. Each of these openings makes clear the tone and content of the day, and hooks student interest or at least their curiosity right away.

Even more engaging is to combine a piece of music with some slides. Imagine, for example, walking into the first class of the first half of the United States history survey hearing Dvorak's *New World Symphony* while looking at slides of

American Indians. Although few students these days know Dvorak's music, the dissonance of the classical tones with images of Indians arouses immediate interest and raises questions before a word has been spoken. The first words of the class invite students to suggest all the things wrong with the sentence, "Columbus discovered America in 1492." Within the hour shift to Neil Diamond singing "America," as students view slides of immigrants, "boat people," streaming to the United States from all over the world. His refrain, "we come to America," leads to a discussion of who Americans are and where they came from and how and why. The earlier discussion of Native Americans becomes unavoidably a part of the explorations.

The combination of slides and songs can be used again later in the term to illustrate slavery (with spirituals and blues) and the Civil War. Imagine looking at battlefield scenes while listening to "We are Coming, Father Abraham" or George Frederick Root's "Battle Cry of Freedom." Or, more poignantly, imagine the combination of slides of gutted, demolished, southern cities while listening to "Dixie" and "Marching Through Georgia." Or consider the evocative power of showing scenes of young Civil War soldiers, North and South, alive, dying, and dead, while listening to "Just Before the Battle, Mother," "The Drummer Boy of Shiloh," and "Johnny Comes Marching Home."

Even more powerful is to synchronize one or two slides with each lyrical line of a song. For "Tenting on the Old Camp Ground," for example, show slides of tent camps and tired but hopeful soldiers to accompany such lines as "We're tenting tonight on the old Camp ground / Give us a song to cheer / Our weary hearts, a song of home / And friends we love so dear. / Tenting tonight / Tenting tonight / Tenting on the old Camp ground."

Rather than lecturing on the overall battle strategies of the North and South during the Civil War, which are usually covered well in textbooks, I prefer to make a slide and music presentation and then deal in some detail with only one strategically crucial battle, say, Chickamauga, where 34,000 died in two days. Students understand the unbelievable human and physical devastation of the Civil War with their hearts and emotions as well as with their heads and reason.

The possibilities for the twentieth century are obviously much more extensive. For example, imagine the effect of listening to Elton John's "All Quiet on the Western Front" while looking at scenes of World War I trenches, or Billy Joel's "Goodnight Saigon" while viewing slides of American soldiers and Vietnamese peasants. There are many effective combinations of labor songs and struggle, or of civil rights songs with scenes of the movement and the resistance against it. Or use speeches, again with visual slide images. To show the shift in the mood of the black liberation struggle in the mid-1960s, compare Malcolm X's "Message to the Grass Roots," delivered in November 1963, with Dr. Martin Luther King's "I Have a Dream" speech three months earlier. Even more powerfully, put some slides together synchronized with the visual images suggested during the last five minutes of Dr. King's Memphis speech in the evening of April 3, 1968, "I See the Promised Land . . . I've Been to the Mountaintop," concluding with images of King's assassination and funeral.

The singer, Harry Chapin, who also died tragically too young a few years ago, wrote and performed songs that told poignantly human stories of ordinary people's everyday struggles and tragedies. He also sang of the changes from the 1960s to the 1970s. "She Is Always Seventeen" presents a metaphoric story of broken and persisting dreams while moving historically through the period from 1961 ("when we went to Washington . . . And said, 'Camelot's begun'") to 1975 ("when the crooked king was gone . . . [we were] sayin, 'the dream must go on.'"). After listening to a slide-tape of this song, ask students, "Which visual image or lyrical line moved you the most?" and then, perhaps in pairs, to consider the question of "the meaning of the chorus and title."

After exploring students' immediate emotional responses to Chapin's, or any other song, it is helpful to go back through the piece again slowly, slide by slide, discussing the historical context and meaning of each line of lyrics and how it is further illuminated by the visual image that accompanies it.

The use of music and slides, though presentational, is an intensely active experience for students. But the use of powerful emotion in class raises significant questions of power and freedom in the classroom. The emotions that are evoked are overwhelming as we hear Dr. King conclude his "Mountaintop" speech with the words, "Mine eyes have seen the glory of the coming of the Lord," and the visual image of King shifts from a lectern to the balcony of the Memphis motel. The intensity of emotion is palpable and I am aware that, after an excruciatingly long moment of silence to let the image sink in, whatever I choose to say next, if anything at all, has enormous power to be deeply heard and retained. It is a humbling responsibility, suggesting the need to make quiet and gently understated comments about justice and the meaning of Dr. King's life. Or better yet, ask students to write for a minute or two, and then talk with the person next to them before we intrude with thoughts or questions.

Emotions are a powerfully affective learning strategy and we need to learn how to deal with student feelings as well as their intellect in responding to music and slides (and films). We do not abuse our responsibility if we respect the students' need for personal space to absorb the experience. Quiet writing time and talking in pairs can provide this space. Sometimes it is best to let the music and slides make the whole point, without our comment, and just simply conclude the class. Let the students leave with whatever each individual carries away in his or her heart and head from the experience. This guarantees that they will own their feelings and insights.

The last point has been the pervasive theme of this article. The key to effective learning, the kind that is both lasting and transforming, is in empowering students through various strategies of active involvement to own their own learning. Emerson once wrote in his journal that a wise person "must feel and teach that the best wisdom cannot be communicated [but] must be acquired by every soul for itself." In each of the teaching strategies suggested here, I have sought to show that large impersonal lecture hall classes need not be barriers to providing the kind of interactive, investigative, and even intimate experiences that enhance student learning.

What is more difficult to show is how to balance the time it takes for active learning activities from the imperative to "cover" as much material as possible in each class. It is inherent in being an historian to make choices about what to select, or cover. In our writing we are always selecting themes and events to emphasize, thus leaving out something else. As teachers, too, we choose whether to spend a given 10- to 15-minute block of class time for a writing exercise, or to analyze a document or painting, or to create small groups to decide an historical question, or to lecture on, say, mercantilism, or the party battles of the 1830s, or money policy in the 1870s, or men's responses to feminism. Our choices depend on our goals as teachers, on what kinds of students we want to turn out, on how we have resolved what we think are the essential questions and irreducibly significant facts and concepts of our field, and to some extent on institutional mission. As economists would say, "It's a trade-off," and we all make our own difficult choices.

I have chosen to give up "covering" mercantilism, the Specie Circular, the Dingley Tariff, and many other events, for example, in return for more interaction among students, more writing and close analysis of primary documents in class, including the crucial documents of American history, and more use of visuals and music to evoke emotions. And I spend twice as long as I used to on the experiences of women and minorities. I also give map questions on every test. These choices are made clear to me by my goals, which begin fundamentally with structuring ways of empowering students to discover, and own, historical knowledge, skills, and attitudes for themselves and to feel good about themselves as learners. Bolstering student self-esteem in a history class makes it more likely that students' knowledge of history will be increased and their motivation for further learning will be intensified. Who knows, with more options for actively involving students in the learning of history, Henry Adams might have stayed in teaching.

NOTES

1. See also Diane Ravitch. (November 17, 1985). "Decline and Fall of Teaching History." *New York Times Magazine,* 50-56, 101, 117.

2. See especially, Arthur W. Chickering and Zelda F. Gamson. (March 1987). Seven Principles for Good Practice in Undergraduate Education. *AAHE Bulletin; Involvement in Learning: Realizing the Potential of American Higher Education.* (October 1984). National Institute of Education; Ernest L. Boyer. (1987). *College: The Undergraduate Experience in America.* (The Carnegie Foundation for the Advancement of Teaching). New York: Harper & Row; *A New Vitality in General Education.* (1988). Association of American Colleges.

REFERENCES

Adams, H. (1918). *The Education of Henry Adams.* Boston: Houghton Mifflin Co., 300-304.

Hoff-Wilson, J. (May 1986). Report of the Executive Secretary. *OAH Newsletter:* 1.

McGregor, D. K. & McGregor, R. K. (May 1988). Strange brew 'new' history and old methods. *OAH Newsletter:* 10-11.

Morgan, E. S. (1958). *The Puritan Dilemma: The Story of John Winthrop.* Boston: Little, Brown and Company.

Taylor, G. R., ed. (1950s-1960s). *Problems in American Civilization.* (title series). Boston: D.C. Heath.

Thelen, D. (June 1986). The professor and *The Journal of American History. The Journal of American History* 73: 9.

Weisberger, B. A. (February/March 1987). American history is falling down. *American Heritage:* 32.

PART III

ASSESSMENT

Assessing collaborative learning and Cooperative Learning activities is an important topic for a classroom teacher in the public schools. Assessment is even more important, however for higher education faculty since the contact hours with students are dramatically reduced due to the nature of the courses.

Carol B. Furtwengler discusses the elements that are necessary in assessing the Cooperative Learning process. She states that the Cooperative Learning assessment process must demonstrate three fundamental concepts: (a) group accountability, (b) individual accountability, and (c) positive interdependence among group members. She provides a tripartite grading system that incorporates these concepts and evaluative forms that support this system.

Tara S. Azwell provides specific assessment strategies, which necessarily must differ depending on the purpose of the assessment and the product or process being assessed. She states that there are three key issues that must be addressed. She points out that the terms *assessment, evaluation,* and *grading* are used interchangeably by many instructors but that there are very important differences in their meanings.

Higher education faculty members are concerned about assessment and evaluation issues. This section links assessment and evaluation to cooperative and collaborative learning strategies.

10

PRACTICAL METHODS FOR ASSESSING COOPERATIVE LEARNING IN HIGHER EDUCATION

by Carol B. Furtwengler

Higher education faculty members who want to use Cooperative Learning in their classrooms often have concerns about the assessment of student group work and its relationship to individual grades. This chapter provides practical methods for the assessment of Cooperative Learning in higher education and begins with an overview of the research on Cooperative Learning in kindergarten through twelfth grade (K-12) education and higher education. Major barriers to the use of Cooperative Learning in higher education are explored, and a rationale is provided for the support of this instructional strategy in college classrooms. Basic concepts of Cooperative Learning are outlined, and these concepts are used as a framework for suggested methods to assess student progress and performance. The chapter concludes with a self-assessment checklist for higher education faculty members to use in evaluating and improving their Cooperative Learning teaching strategies.

THE RESEARCH BASE

Cooperative Learning as a teaching strategy has become commonplace in K-12 classrooms and is recognized as a teaching methodology with far-reaching benefits for classrooms of the future (Glickman, 1992). Confidence in the use of Cooperative Learning in K-12 education is supported by an extensive research base that demonstrates this method's effectiveness in improving students' academic achievement and social skills (Foyle, Lyman, & Morehead, 1989). Slavin (1988) reports wide acceptance of the belief that "cooperative methods can and usually do have a positive effect on student achievement" (p. 52). A meta-analysis of 122 studies conducted by Johnson, Maruyama, Johnson, Nelson, and Skon (1981) reveals that "the overall effects stand as strong evidence for the superiority of cooperation in promoting achievement and productivity" (p. 58).

Two other leading proponents of Cooperative Learning, Johnson and Johnson (1983), focus primarily on the social aspects of Cooperative Learning. They state: "Cooperative Learning experiences, where students work together to maximize each other's achievement, tend also to promote positive relationships and a process of acceptance among students" (p. 22). Brandt (1990) reports that Cooperative Learning leads to a "more pro-social orientation," and his synthesis indicates "tremendous improvements in social relations" (p. 8). A study by Johnson, Johnson, and Scott (1978) suggests that Cooperative Learning promotes interpersonal liking, attraction, trust, a sense of being accepted by teachers and peers, and more positive attitudes toward school and learning than does either competitive or individualistic instruction. Further, another study by Johnson and Johnson (1983) indicates that when Cooperative Learning is used, students work together to help each other learn, have positive general and school-related self-esteem, and feel worthwhile as persons and competent as students. Other benefits from Cooperative Learning include increases in student attendance and motivation (Slavin, 1987).

Recent research on the use of Cooperative Learning in higher education reveals similar findings to the research from K-12 education. Johnson and Johnson (1987) report increased achievement, positive interpersonal relationships, social support and self-esteem among adults who participate in Cooperative Learning. Other researchers (Courtney, Courtney, & Nicholson, 1992) report that Cooperative Learning positively influences student motivation, self-efficacy, level of anxiety, and sense of social cohesiveness. Glass and Putnam (1989) report that students rate Cooperative Learning more favorably than lecture-discussion activities and believe that student perceptions indicate that Cooperative Learning may make the university classroom more productive and intellectually stimulating. Millis (1990) found that Cooperative Learning is more effective, more "fun," and leads to greater student involvement and cooperative group skills. She believes that "cooperative learning can positively affect student learners, faculty, and the general campus climate" (p. 53). Dansereau (1983) reports the results of three experiments with students in retention of main ideas from expository texts using Cooperative Learning pairs. He found that students who worked in cooperative pairs out-performed students who studied alone. The research base for the use of Cooperative Learning in higher education is an emerging, promising field. Many faculty members, however, remain uncomfortable using the basic tenets of Cooperative Learning.

BARRIERS TO COOPERATIVE LEARNING

Major barriers to the use of Cooperative Learning exist in higher education. First, teaching skill is often taken for granted in higher education. In spite of the fact that effective classroom instruction is included in performance evaluations, department chairpersons, associate deans, and faculty peers rarely visit classrooms. The most common feedback on teaching performance comes from student evaluations, which are done only when required by the institution and/or desired by the professor. Second, there is little encouragement for professors to explore new teaching methods. Staff development funds for learning new teaching strategies are nearly nonexistent. Opportunities for "in-service" training, therefore, are usually limited to professional meetings and conventions. Third, professors have grown up in a climate of "academic competition." Maintaining high grade-point averages when they were in college meant listening carefully to lectures, taking accurate notes, and recalling and applying the knowledge on a written examination. It is natural for faculty members to model what they know, and that, in most instances, is a directed teaching style. Comfortable with this style, professors tend to question how grades will be assigned to individuals who participate in group efforts. Guidelines for assessing these group efforts are unclear, and professors may feel that a "one student, one grade" approach is more equitable. In spite of these barriers, there is evidence that Cooperative Learning is an appropriate strategy for higher education and that individual and group efforts can be effectively evaluated.

Basic Concepts of Cooperative Learning

Leading researchers on Cooperative Learning have defined the basic concepts inherent in this teaching and learning method. To improve achievement through Cooperative Learning, two conditions are necessary: a group goal and individual accountability for each group member. When these conditions are met, as is shown in Slavin's (1988) review of Cooperative Learning literature, substantial gains in achievement occur. Students in groups stressing group goals and individual accountability achieved significantly higher than groups stressing only one or neither of these conditions.

The concepts used in reference to Cooperative Learning (Johnson & Johnson, 1994; Johnson, Johnson, & Holubec, 1991) represent the pedagogical base for assessment strategies. These concepts are:

Positive interdependence. Students must believe that they are responsible for their own learning and the learning of the other members of their group.

Face-to-face promotive interaction. Students must have the opportunity to explain what they are learning to each other and to help each other understand and complete assignments.

Individual accountability. Students must individually demonstrate mastery of the assigned work.

Social skills. Students must communicate effectively, provide leadership for their group's work, build and maintain trust among members, and resolve conflicts within their group constructively.

Group processing. Groups must stop periodically and assess how well they are working and how their effectiveness may be improved.

The traditional learning approach used in most classrooms works against these Cooperative Learning concepts.

Group work usually provides no individual accountability, no student interdependence, and no group processing skills. Social skills are usually understood, rather than taught as part of the curriculum. Differences between traditional and Cooperative Learning groups, based on work of Johnson, Johnson, Holubec, and Roy (1984), are shown in Figure 10.1.

Figure 10.1
Comparison of Cooperative Learning to Traditional Group Work

Cooperative Groups	Traditional Groups
Positive interdependence	No interdependence
Heterogeneous membership	Homogeneous membership
Shared leadership	One appointed leader
Responsible for each other	Responsible only for self
Social skills directly taught	Social skills assumed and ignored
Teacher observes and intervenes	Teacher ignores groups
Group processing occurs	No group processing occurs

This comparison highlights the importance of group members being dependent on each other for the group's success. Instead of students being structured in a competitive mode, where they benefit from other students' incorrect answers, they feel responsible as a team member for the learning of each student. An incorrect response is a reflection on the learning of the group rather than the inability of an individual student.

Assessing Cooperative Learning: The Tripartite Method

The Cooperative Learning assessment process must demonstrate three fundamental concepts: (a) achievement of the group goal, (b) individual accountability, and (c) positive interdependence among group members. A tripartite grading system incorporates these concepts. Cooperative Learning groups are informed at the initiation of the projects that grades will be assigned using three assessment methods. Each method has equal weight in determining the final grade for the Cooperative Learning project.

Group Accountability

The teacher evaluates the final project and this constitutes one-third of the grade. Projects can vary based on subject area and teacher objectives. Examples of possible projects include (a) creating handbooks for the entire class on selected course topics that will be of practical use to students after completion of the course, (b) writing a concise outline of study notes on a particular area to be used in a Jigsaw situation, (c) producing a videotape on a major course topic, or (d) performing a class role-play to demonstrate important class objectives. Students in the author's educational administration classes have used all of these methods successfully in Cooperative Learning projects. Handbooks for school administrators have been developed on topics such as "Assisting the Beginning Teacher," "Crisis Management in the School," and "Special Education Inclusion Programs." Student groups have created videotapes that demonstrate clinical supervision conferencing skills and mentoring programs for beginning teachers. Cooperative groups have role-played a teacher dismissal case from the teacher's initial meeting with the principal through a court appeal.

The final group accountability grade for the project is based on whether the project (a) met its stated goals, (b) was technically accurate (content, grammar, writing), (c) was shared and presented in a manner that helped all students to learn, and (d) demonstrated appropriate effort and coverage of the topic.

Individual Accountability

The teacher examines the student's Cooperative Learning Log and this constitutes one-third of the Cooperative

Learning grade. Figure 10.2 displays a Cooperative Learning Log kept by students. It requires the student to record the date and outside-of-class time spent (in hours) on the project and explain the activity (e.g., conducting library searches, reviewing literature, meeting with fellow group members, and writing, editing, and producing the final product). The product from the activity (if applicable) is stapled to the log and numbered. For instance, if the student has completed a library search, this material is attached to the log and marked as Exhibit 1. Students keep the log throughout the cooperative group project, and the teacher grades the log and attached material. The teacher examines the final report and compares each person's individual effort to determine his or her contribution to the final project.

Positive Interdependence

The teacher requires each member of the cooperative group to grade other team members based on their contribution to the group goal. Figure 10.3 shows the performance rating sheet with its six specific areas for judgment of performance. In addition to judging the six areas, students assign an overall project grade with specific rationale for that grade for each individual team member, including themselves. This process is one way to use peer evaluation and to promote positive interdependence at the beginning of the project. Students know that they have a responsibility to each member of the group. It is the group's responsibility to see that all members are productive participants and share equally in the project.

These three grades that represent group accountability, individual accountability, and positive interdependence are then averaged by the teacher to determine the final grade for the Cooperative Learning activity. A last step in the assessment project also addresses positive interdependence. A question is included on the final examination pertaining to the Cooperative Learning project. The question is individualized for each Cooperative Learning group. Teams are told before the examination that a question unique to their particular project will be part of the examination. Students are allowed 30

Figure 10.2
Cooperative Learning Log

Name:_____   Class:_____

Cooperative Group:_____

Date	Time Spent (Hours)	Specific Activity	Product of Activity (Attach if applicable)	No. of Exhibit

Figure 10.3
Cooperative Learning Team Member
Performance Rating Sheet

Name of Cooperative Learning Team
Member:_____

Class:_____

Rate each of the following statements using the following scale:

        5 - Strongly Agree
        4 - Agree
        3 - Neither Agree nor Disagree
        2 - Disagree
        1 - Strongly Disagree

1. This team member provided appropriate   1 2 3 4 5
   leadership for our group.

2. This team member completed assigned tasks.   1 2 3 4 5

3.This team member arrived promptly at meetings   1 2 3 4 5
   and met the team's deadlines.

4. This team member used facilitative (helping, listening,   1 2 3 4
   5
   encouraging, sharing, providing directions) behavior
   during cooperative work.

5. This team member shared information and   1 2 3 4 5
   materials to help others.

6. This team member contributed to the quality and   1 2 3 4 5
   success of the team's project/activity.

I would assign this team member the following grade based on the
specific, objective data provided below:

minutes of in-class time prior to the examination date to study together to reinforce the concept of positive interdependence.

Assessing Cooperative Learning Through a Reflective Student Log

Another strategy for assessing Cooperative Learning that is often appropriate, particularly at the advanced graduate level, is the use of a reflective student log. Students with advanced graduate status may have higher levels of involvement in Cooperative Learning projects. This participation includes extensive projects that may last more than a semester.

The author participates in a field-based, applied inquiry Ed.D. program in educational administration where students conduct studies for local school districts as members of research teams. During this process, the professors observe students as they work in groups and teach group process and interpersonal relations are taught during seminar interactions. The professors in this program work closely with small cohorts of students and serve as members of the research team. They are, therefore, aware on a weekly basis of each student's performance and contribution to the project's goals, the positive interdependence of the team, and the importance of group accountability in providing a final product of high quality.

An essential component of the Ed.D. program is a reflective student log created by each degree candidate during program participation. Students are encouraged to write the log in a frank and honest manner. Ideas and feelings are accepted regardless of the viewpoints. This log is an important assessment tool in determining students' academic and social progress. The log requires weekly entries in four sections:

Section I. Class session or field work: provides an accurate account of what occurred during classroom seminars or cooperative, field-based research projects.

Section II. Reaction: includes thoughts and feelings about the class. This entry indicates (a) an understanding of the purpose of the class, (b) consideration of its meaning to the individual and group, (c) a response to the social interactions of the class, and (d) an awareness of reasons for personal feelings about the class.

Section III. Preparation: provides a specific record of class preparation. This entry includes (a) readings, (b) preparation of class materials and assignments, and (c) mental preparation (thought processes) for class and field assignments.

Section IV. Conclusions: includes tentative conclusions about the course to date. This brings together all the readings, discussions, and cooperative research studies of the class. This section reveals major understandings and progress toward class objectives.

Criteria for assessing the log require that all four entries are present each week. A five-point rating scale is used to determine the degree of information contained in the log from (1) superficial and sketchy to (5) reveals excellent insight. The thoroughness of descriptions is rated from (1) too brief to (5) very thorough. Students are provided feedback on their increased understanding of course content, group dynamics, and team work.

All professors teaching on the cohort team review each student's log and attempt to provide critical and supportive feedback. When students first record information in the logs, they may not provide enough reflection or may not be able to reveal their personal feelings about the course content and their ability to work in a seminar and team setting. Comments of professors may include notes such as "reflective thinking not apparent," "feelings not reported," "purpose not understood," "outside of class reflection not reported," "classes and reading not integrated" and "conclusions not unified." Conversely, as students progress in their academic work and understanding of group dynamics and team work, their logs include positive comments by professors. As students progress in making log entries throughout their degree program, they become more skilled in sharing their personal and social learning through the reflective process. These logs provide data for the professors and, when combined with in-class and field observations, serve as an assessment tool for cooperative team efforts. These data also allow for the assessment of the professors' performance, since logs often contain recommendations for changes in class structure and cooperative work.

This rich data source is an excellent assessment tool for understanding academic and social progress in a Cooperative Learning environment. These data allow for assessment of student progress and assessment of the professors' performance. Students soon learn to be frank and honest and offer suggestions or reflections on ways to improve seminar team work and/or cooperative field studies.

A Self-Assessment Checklist

Higher education faculty members can evaluate their own Cooperative Learning instruction using a checklist that reflects, with some modification, the major research on the effectiveness of this instructional strategy. The teacher's goal should be multifaceted and should address the underlying principles for using Cooperative Learning: (a) what are the course content objectives that I want to achieve through cooperative team work? (b) what are the social skills I want students to practice and learn through Cooperative Learning activities? and (c) how am I preparing my students for today's workplace, which replaces individual competition with team effort?

A checklist for the self-assessment of Cooperative Learning is provided in Figure 10.4. This checklist is adapted from previous work that identifies criteria for the observation of Cooperative Learning classrooms (Furtwengler, 1993; Furtwengler, 1992). Elements on the checklist criteria are defined below.

Clearly defined goals and objectives. The teacher has determined the instructional goals (both academic and social) that will be achieved through the cooperative process.

A rationale for group size and composition. Group size can vary depending upon the task. Research reveals, however, that for Cooperative Learning to be most successful,

Figure 10.4
Cooperative Learning Self-Assessment Checklist

The Teacher:

_____ defines goal and objectives clearly.

_____ establishes rationale for group size and composition.

_____ provides appropriate physical space for group work.

_____ assures that materials are available and shared.

_____ establishes clear guidelines.

_____ explains clearly grading and project procedures.

_____ establishes a class time line for cooperative activities.

_____ maintains awareness of each group's progress toward goal attainment.

_____ provides opportunity to learn social skills.

_____ help students with conflict resolution.

_____ provides methods to assess positive interdependence among group members and group and individual accountability.

_____ monitors the cooperative learning process by noting progress and problems.

_____ utilizes reteaching and classroom discussion when appropriate.

_____ provides innovative formats to share cooperative learning activities/projects.

_____ provides an opportunity for students to reflect on their effective-ness.

_____ reflects on the cooperative learning instruction and assesses things that went well and things that need modification.

groups of from two to six members are most effective. The groups should be heterogeneous based upon academic ability, race, and gender. In higher education, unique criteria exist that may affect the creation of heterogeneous groups. First, most students are more self-initiating in their learning and usually predetermine their areas of interest if given a choice of assignments. This allows students to select their own groups rather than allowing the teacher an opportunity to create heterogeneity among the groups. Second, the students' proximity to one another is an issue in higher education due to work schedules, commuting students, and available transportation. Third, if the higher education institution maintains qualified admissions standards, the academic ability of the students may not provide a broad range of difference among students. Finally, with many returning students in today's college classroom, age can also be a factor in determining group heterogeneity. The teacher should consider all of these variables during preparation for Cooperative Learning activities.

Physical space. For Cooperative Learning to be successful, space must be available for all group members to see and hear one another when participating in Cooperative Learning activities. As the project expands, the students bring reference materials and information (textbooks, articles, videotapes, and artifacts) to class that require additional room. The ideal classroom consists of a large room with work tables and provides enough space between groups to minimize distractions. Separate rooms allow for more privacy and fewer distractions for team members but limit the teacher's ability to observe and monitor group work effectively.

Provision of materials. In Cooperative Learning, teachers become facilitators. Instead of teaching from a textbook, all team members become resources and the teacher becomes a "sharer" of information. The philosophy changes from "it is your project and your responsibility to seek out information" to one of "I can serve as a resource to your team, and we can help each other locate what we need."

Clear guidelines. The teacher establishes guidelines that facilitate positive interdependence and promote group unity/harmony. It is clear that everyone must contribute, help, listen with care to others, encourage others to participate, and ask for help or clarification.

Clear grading and project procedures. The teacher provides students with clear instructions for the use of the Cooperative Learning log and explains that each individual must keep an accurate record of activities and projects to be submitted with the final report. The teacher provides expectations for journals if students are using reflective journals. the teacher also provides students with a copy of the rating sheet for evaluating each team member's work and explains their responsibility for contributing to individual and group accountability and positive interdependence.

A class time line for cooperative activities. Students in higher education are expected to do "homework" and spend at least twice the amount of in-class time on assignments. It is important, however, for the teacher to observe and monitor group work and to be aware of the progress each group is making on their cooperative projects. Throughout the semester (or allotted time frame), the teacher should schedule class time for team work. Students should know in advance on what specific days instructional time will be provided for the Cooperative Learning project.

Monitoring of each group's progress toward goal achievement. By allowing class time for cooperative team work, the teacher can monitor and assess each group's process and products. Other strategies for checking progress are to let each team report weekly on their project or, if the project is extensive, to collect logs several times during the semester to assess individual progress.

Opportunity to learn social skills. The teacher is aware of group process skills and provides opportunities for students to learn social skills. An important part of goal achievement is the social skills that students gain through Cooperative Learning. The teacher can make this an interesting part of the class by having students discuss their interactions, their problems, and their successes. Most students in higher education classes today have little experience with team learning and are initially more comfortable with a competitive mode. They need opportunities to vent frustrations, share successes, and look at alternative strategies for problem solving as they experience this new way of learning.

Help with conflict resolution. The teacher must be prepared to intervene if groups are unable to resolve issues or come to an impasse regarding decisions about their project. The teacher becomes a fact finder and mediator and through paraphrasing and problem solving allows groups to overcome the barriers to their success.

Methods to assess positive interdependence among group members and group and individual accountability. The tripartite method, the final examination, and the reflective student log are assessment tools the teacher can use to provide accountability for Cooperative Learning. Other methods to use for accountability, observation, and monitoring of group work are:

Monitoring of the Cooperative Learning process by noting progress and problems. The teacher circulates during Cooperative Learning activities, making note of individual and group accomplishments, how progress is being made toward goal attainment, and how problems are being resolved. Monitoring focuses on whether the students understand the assignment and materials. The teacher provides task assistance by clarifying, reteaching, and elaborating, if necessary. The teacher also lets students know when they are making progress.

Reteaching and classroom discussion. The teacher uses notes from monitoring of groups' progress and from student and group input to identify areas that need reteaching or further class discussion. As the groups formalize their answers or complete their projects, the teacher reviews the answers and products. If there are problems or incorrect material, the teacher uses this opportunity to reteach or discuss the correct information with the group. If problems occur in group interaction or work process, the teacher also reviews and reteaches the social skills necessary to increase group cohesiveness and effectiveness.

Innovative formats to share Cooperative Learning results. Upon completion of their project, students need an opportunity to share their learning with others in the class. The teacher should promote innovative formats for presentation of group projects, such as conducting a radio or television talk show allowing "viewer" call-ins from other class members, viewing a group-produced videotape, or conducting a role-play emphasizing major learning from the group's work.

Opportunity for students to reflect on their own effectiveness. Cooperative Learning is often a new process for university students. At the conclusion of each Cooperative Learning lesson or project, students should share their successes and failures as a group, thus allowing all students to learn from their mistakes. Reflecting on their effectiveness can increase achievement, extend students' thinking to higher-order skills, and allow creative problem solving among students. Sample questions to pose to groups include: What did work and what did not work? Why? What went well and what needs revision or improvement? What would we do differently next time? What did we learn and understand about our task or project?

Teacher reflection and assessment of the Cooperative Learning instruction. After the students have completed their assessment, the teacher notes successes and methods for improving the teaching of Cooperative Learning and then uses these notes when planning the next course.

Conclusion

The research literature shows positive evidence that Cooperative Learning is an effective instructional methodology. Personnel in higher education are often leery, however, of Cooperative Learning techniques. One of the reasons for this reluctance is the concern about the assessment of individual progress when students work on a group project.

This chapter has outlined several assessment techniques for Cooperative Learning activities. The first uses a tripartite approach basing grades upon the basic concepts inherent in Cooperative Learning: individual responsibility through the Cooperative Learning log, group responsibility through assessment of the final project, and positive interdependence through group assessment of each member's learning. The final examination is another avenue for using reinforcement of positive interdependence by requiring students to study together for a question on their group project. Another evaluation strategy is the use of a reflective journal that allows students to record four entries each week that provide assessment data for the teacher.

Finally, teachers can assess their own performance by reviewing the Cooperative Learning Self-Assessment Checklist. This provides a self-assessment process for the teacher and allows the teacher to continue to improve teaching strategies for Cooperative Learning in the higher education classroom.

REFERENCES

Brandt, R. (1990). On cooperative learning: A conversation with Spencer Kagan. *Educational Leadership* 47(4): 8-11.

Courtney, D. P., Courtney, M., & Nicholson, C. (1992). "The Effect of Cooperative Learning as an Instructional Practice at the College Level." Paper presented at the annual meeting of the Mid-South Educational Research Association, Knoxville, TN.

Dansereau, D. F. (1983). *Cooperative learning: Impact on acquisition of knowledge and skills.* (Technical Report No. 586). Fort Worth: Texas Christian University. (ERIC Document Reproduction Service No. ED 243 088.)

Foyle, H. C., Lyman, L., & Morehead, M. A. (1989). "Interactive Learning: Creating an Environment for Cooperative Learning." Paper presented at the annual conference of the Association for Supervision and Curriculum Development, Orlando, FL.

Furtwengler, C. (1992). How to observe cooperative learning classrooms. *Educational Leadership* 49(7): 59-63.

————. (1993). *"Observing Cooperative Learning Classrooms: A Research Based Formative Observation Instrument."* Paper presented at the annual meeting of the American Educational Research Association, Atlanta, GA.

Glass, R. M., & Putnam, J. (1989). Cooperative learning in teacher education: A case study. *Action in Teacher Education* 10(4): 47-52.

Glickman, C. D. (1992). The essence of school renewal: The prose has begun. *Educational Leadership* 50(1): 24-27.

Johnson, D. W., & Johnson, R. T. (1983). Effects of cooperative, competitive, and individualistic learning experiences on social development. *Exceptional Children* 49: 323-29.

————. (1987). Research shows the benefits of adult cooperation. *Educational Leadership* 45(3): 27-30.

————. (1994). *Learning Together and Alone: Cooperative, Competitive, & Individualistic Learning.* 4th ed. Boston: Allyn and Bacon.

Johnson, D. W., Johnson, R. T., & Holubec, E. J. (1991). *Cooperation in the Classroom.* rev. ed. Edina, MN: Interaction Book Company.

Johnson, D. W., Johnson, R. T. Holubec, E. J., & Roy, P. (1984). *Circles of Learning: Cooperation in the Classroom.* Alexandria, VA: Association for Supervision and Curriculum Development.

Johnson, D. W., Johnson, R. T., & Scott. A. (1978). The effects of cooperative and individualized instruction on student attitudes and achievement. *Journal of Social Psychology* 104: 207-16.

Johnson, D. W., Maruyama, G., Johnson, R. T., Nelson, D., & Skon, L. (1981). Effect of cooperative, competitive and individualistic goal structure on achievement: A meta-analysis. *Psychological Bulletin* 89: 47-62.

Millis, B. J. (1990). Helping faculty building learning communities through cooperative groups. *To Improve the Academy* 9: 43-58.

Slavin, R. E. (1987). Cooperative learning and the cooperative school. *Educational Leadership* 45(3): 7-13.
————. Cooperative learning and student achievement. *Educational Leadership* 46(2): 31-33.

————. (1990). *Cooperative Learning: Theory, Research, and practice.* Englewood Cliffs, NJ: Prentice-Hall.

11

ALTERNATIVE ASSESSMENT FORMS

by Tara S. Azwell

College students are like all students. They construct their knowledge through social interaction. They bring widely varying levels of prior knowledge to any learning experience. They have varying learning styles. They maximize their learning when participating in authentic learning activities. They begin by approximating the desired performance and refining their knowledge and skill over time as they move toward higher levels of competency. And like all students, they require different amounts of time to reach similar levels of competence.

College teachers read such statements and reply, "Of course," but the instructional and assessment strategies employed in most college classes are not congruent with what is known about the ways many students learn. A major question remains: How can grades be fairly assigned when students investigate different questions, develop different products, spend different amounts of time learning, and work in different social configurations? This chapter will describe some assessment strategies that can be used in collaborative learning activities.

Important Questions About Assessment

College students collaborate in many ways. They collaborate to gain higher levels of understanding of the concepts and relationships within a course. They collaborate to improve their ability to work with others. They collaborate to improve their communication skills. They collaborate to produce products.

Assessment strategies must differ depending on the purpose of the assessment and the product or process being assessed. To discuss assessment strategies that can be used in

160

collaborative learning activities three key issues must be addressed:

- What are the definitions of *assessment, evaluation,* and *grading?*
- What are the purposes of assessment, evaluation, and grading?
- What are the characteristics of effective assessment, evaluation, and grading?

Defining the Terms

Although the terms *assessment, evaluation,* and *grading* are used interchangeably by many instructors, there are very important differences in meaning. Assessment is used to describe the gathering of information about the level of knowledge or performance. Evaluation is the determination of the meaning of the information that was gathered. Formative evaluation occurs during the learning process and provides feedback to the learner about the accuracy of the learning or about the level of performance. Summative evaluation occurs at the end of the learning sequence to determine if the curricular outcome was met. Grading attempts to sort the performance into a scale or series.

Purposes of Assessment, Evaluation, and Grading

Assessment, evaluation and grading, while being very different concepts, share some common purposes. Herman, Aschbacher, and Winters (1992, p.2) said that assessment and evaluation "hold educators to set standards, create instructional pathways, motivate performance, provide diagnostic feedback, assess/evaluate progress, and communicate progress to others." Assessment, evaluation, and grading are each helpful for several of these purposes. They are all used at different points within the learning process.

Characteristics of Effective Assessment, Evaluation, and Grading

Anthony, Johnson, Mickelson, and Prece (1991) describe principles that apply to effective assessment and evaluation programs. Effective assessment and evaluation should be centered in the classroom, be consistent with curricular goals, be consistent with what is known about human learning, and be comprehensive and balanced. To accomplish these ends, all assessment and evaluation procedures must be:

- numerous,
- multifaceted (occurring in varied ways),
- lead to profiles of growth and achievement over time,
- qualitative as well as quantitative,
- reflective of the "constructive" nature of learning,
- collaborative (focused upon the judgment of all concerned),
- noncompetitive (focused on individual achievement rather than on comparative data),
- positive and helpful in leading to the growth of the learner,
- adaptive (shaped to fit the particular circumstances).

These views of effective assessment and evaluation match closely the rationale for involving learners in collaborative activities.

To be effective, assessment and evaluation must also be reliable, valid, authentic and focused on what the student knows (Anthony et al., 1991; Herman et al., 1992). Effective assessment and evaluation must encourage in-depth learning. They should examine both the processes and products of learning.

Traditionally, the purpose of assessment and evaluation in many college classes has been to assign a grade instead of to help students move toward mastery of an outcome goal. New paradigms of learning are causing many college instructors to rethink the purposes for and kinds of assessment/evaluation procedures that they are using.

Assessing Products and Processes

College students collaborate in many ways. No one assessment strategy will effectively measure the knowledge of concepts and relationships, the ability to work with others, the development of communication skills, and the construction of products. A variety of assessment strategies need to be developed in order to monitor learning when students collaborate for so many different purposes.

Assessing the Understanding of Concepts and Relationships

Assessing students' understanding of concepts and relationships through written examination has been the main assessment strategy used in college classes. Traditionally, students were exposed to the material through lectures and assigned readings. They studied for exams alone or formed study groups outside of class. Taking the exam was an individual task done in isolation.

Cooperative Learning strategies such as Think-Pair-Share, Jigsaw, and Group Investigations rely on group responsibility and individual accountability. The assessment procedure following the use of such instructional strategies should be determined by the purpose for the assessment.

If the assessment is used to help students monitor their understanding of the concepts and relationships of the course, the assessment strategy can be a collaborative endeavor also. Students can work together to define terms, solve problems, provide examples, or explain processes. One set of responses is developed by consensus of the group. Groups can then share their responses and discuss the strengths and problems that exist in each response. This type of assessment provides feedback to group members about the level of refinement of their responses. However, if the assessment will be used to assign grades, individually produced quizzes or products should be used. Group "grading" is fraught with negative consequences that actually inhibit the group process.

In the following example of a class activity, students

collaborate to learn the material but are assessed individually. In a teacher education language arts methods class, preservice teachers collaborate to investigate some phase of assessment related to teaching language arts in elementary school. Small groups of three or four students select a facet of assessment to investigate. They read chapters from books and journal articles. They view videotapes. They talk to teachers. Students take notes on what they read or watched. They bring the information back to their small-interest group and share what they have found. Together they develop a short class presentation with a handout to share their study with the entire class. The instructor also shares some information about assessment with students. Following the presentations, each student takes a quiz over assessment strategies for use when teaching language arts.

The quiz is only a small portion of the entire project (thirty of one hundred points). Each individual student receives up to twenty points for the notes from the reading and viewing that they have done in preparation for the group work. The remaining fifty points of the activity come from the presentation and the handout created by the group and the reflection form about the collaborative process. (Figure 11.1 shows the description of the activity in detail and how the activity is evaluated.) Sixty percent of the points for this project were individual points. Fifty of the sixty points specifically related to the assessment of knowledge of content and relationships.

Assessing the Ability to Work with Others

In the group investigations activity described above, one of the assessment tools looked at the development of collaboration skills. To reap the most benefits from collaboration activities (Slavin, 1990), students need to participate in debriefing activities that specifically examine the collaborative process. The Group Assessment Project Evaluation form (see Figure 11.2) is designed for this purpose. Each member of the group completes the form individually. The group discusses the perceptions of members of the group of how the collabo-

Figure 11.1
Cooperative Learning Evaluation Project

By Monday, April 11
    Each person will have read the following material:
        1. Graves - Chapters 27, 28, 29 (pgs. 285-318)
        2. Buchanan - Chapters 8-9 (pgs. 87-143)
        3. One additional article
    Each person will prepare for a cooperative learning group by writing a one-page paper listing two ideas from each of the four articles. The following format is suggested:

    Graves -   Chapter 27
                   1. Idea #l
                   2. Idea #2
    Graves -   Chapter 28
                   1. Idea #l
                   2. Idea #2
    Buchanan -   Chapter 8
                   1. Idea #l
                   2. Idea #2
    Author -   Title
                   1. Idea #l
                   2. Idea #2

    This page of notes may be hand-written. It will be turned in on Monday, April 11. This does not replace your regular log entries. Only those turned in at the end of class are eligible for the 20 points.
    Group members will discuss the material read and plan for a five-minute summary of the group's discussion to be presented on Monday, April 18. The group will prepare a brief handout of no more than 2 pages to share with other class members. Each member of the group should be assigned a responsibility to prepare the handout and the presentation to the class. Each group will be responsible for running of enough copies of their handout for each member of the class to have one.

Evaluation
    This project is worth 100 points. Both group work and individual work will contribute to the 100 points:
        0-20 points Preparation of the one-page paper (individual)
        0-20 points Group presentation (group)
        0-20 points Handout for the class (group)
        0-10 points Self/Group reflection Form (individual and group)
        0-30 points Quiz (individual)
        100 points   TOTAL

rative activity was conducted. They note where the process went well. They also identify ways the group can be more successful in the future. A powerful measure of the ability of the group to collaborate is the frequency of compliments given on the next to the last question. When the last question is answered, the group needs to continue working to develop collaborative skills. In the beginning, students are sometimes hesitant either to give compliments or to discuss problem areas. However, as the level of trust in the group becomes greater, students answer more honestly. Because ten points are given for simply completing the form, students become more comfortable about answering the questions honestly. Honesty and openness, as well as the use of tact, help the group function more successfully.

Assessing Communication Skills

Assessing communication skills is complicated because learners communicate in so many different ways. However, developing the ability to communicate well is one of the prime objectives for most students. Two types of learning activities that involve both collaboration and communication will be described. Assessment strategies for each learning activity will be outlined.

In the collaborative activity described above in which students worked to learn content and relationships and then develop a presentation and handout to share with the whole class, communication was a key issue on several different levels. Figure 11.2 shows how communication was addressed within the collaborative group. Communication was an issue as at least one group member presented the information to the group. Also, the handout conveyed the information through writing and graphics. A rubric for evaluation of both the presentation and the handout was created (see Figure 11.3). A rubric is a fixed scale and a list of characteristics (indicators) describing performance at each level (Marzano, Pickering, & McTighe, 1993). The same rubric was used in both situations. Questions about accuracy, clarity, interest, and mechanics were addressed. Each area was rated on a one to five scale.

Figure 11.2
Group Assessment Project Evaluation

Self-Evaluation

Rate yourself on your performance on the assessment project using the following scale:

Excellent = 5   Good = 4   Fair = 3   Poor = 2   No Contribution = 1

I was prepared to contribute to the group (material read).	5 4 3 2 1
I contributed my ideas.	5 4 3 2 1
I asked others for their ideas.	5 4 3 2 1
I encouraged others to participate in the group.	5 4 3 2 1
I stayed on task.	5 4 3 2 1
I helped others stay on task.	5 4 3 2 1
I did my fair share of the work.	5 4 3 2 1
Overall I feel my performance in the group should be rated:	5 4 3 2 1

Group Evaluation

Rate your group on its performance on the assessment project using the following scale:

Excellent = 5   Good = 4   Fair = 3   Poor = 2   No Contribution = 1

Our group was task-oriented.	5 4 3 2 1
Everyone was prepared (read assigned materials).	5 4 3 2 1
Everyone was encouraged to participate.	5 4 3 2 1
Everyone's quality ideas were respected.	5 4 3 2 1
The quality of our presentation can be described as:	5 4 3 2 1
The qualiy of our handout(s) can be described as:	5 4 3 2 1

Were there members of your group who made exceptional contributions? Who?

_____   _____

_____   _____

Were there members of your group who did not "pull their weight"? Who?

_____   _____

_____   _____

Figure 11.3
Presentation/Handout Rubric

Accuracy of Information

5 All of the information presented was accurate.

4

3 Most of the information presented was accurate, but one or two ideas were misrepresented.

2

1 Most of the information presented was inaccurate.

Clarity

5 The information was clearly presented using understandable vocabulary. Unfamiliar terms were defined or examples of them were given. Good organization helped listeners follow the presentation.

4

3 Most of the information was clearly presented. The use of definitions and/or examples would have been helpful in understanding unfamiliar terms. The material was generally presented in an organized manner.

2

1 Reflection on the Product Form.

Interest

5 The material was presented in an interesting eye-catching or ear-catching manner. The presenter was clearly knowledgeable and interested in the topic.

4

3 Periodically, the presenter aroused the interest of the audience, but much of the information was presented in a bland manner.

2

1 The presenter did little to arouse the interest of the reader or listener. It was obvious that the presenter had little knowledge about or interest in the topic.

Mechanics

5 The presenter used the conventions of speaking and writing. Appearance of the handout or quality of the voice and visual aids was that expected of a knowledgeable professional.

4

3 There were some errors in the use of conventions of speaking and writing. The quality of the handouts or, voice or visual aids was acceptable but not of a professional level.

2

1 Many errors in the use of conventions were noted. The quality of the handouts or, voice or visual aids was not adequate.

The ability to communicate in writing was assessed in another collaborative undertaking. Students took a short-answer essay exam over a unit of study on which they were to demonstrate their understanding of concepts and relationships. Following the exam, two people (the author of the exam and the course instructor) rated the answers using a rubric, that is, standard, indicator, criteria, or descriptor. The essential information that should be included in each answer was described orally by the instructor as the author rated the paper.

A rubric (see Figure 11.4) was then used to evaluate the quality of the written answer using a one to five scale. An answer worth five points contained all of the essential information and was clearly stated. An answer worth three points either contained only part of the essential information or contained all of the information but was not stated clearly. An answer worth one point contained very little of the essential information. Two or four points were given for answers that were somewhere in between the two descriptors. If the ratings of the answers, given by the two raters, differed by more than one point, a

Figure 11.4
Rubric for Rating an Essay Exam

Before using this rubric, identifiiy and share with the student orally or in writing the essential information needed to fully answer each question. It is effective to present the essential information orally as the student rates his or her own exam. This provides an excellent opportunity to review the material one more time when students are listening very carefully. A written version of the essential information can be provided to the second rater to save time.

Each question is rated using the following rubric.

5 All of the essential information is included and is clearly stated.
4
3 Most of the essential information is included and is clearly stated or all of the essential information is included but is not clearly stated.
2
1 Little of the essential information is included or the material is difficult to understand.

third reader was used to resolve the discrepancy. To encourage reflective evaluation, students were given a half-point bonus for each answer that they scored the same as the instructor. Students found that they often knew the material, but had failed to completely and clearly state what they knew.

Assessing Products

Students often collaborate to create products. In fact, the handouts created in the group investigations activity described above is a product. The rubric used to evaluate the handout has already been described.

Students in the language arts methods class were asked to demonstrate their understanding of the theories of language development described by such theorists as Piaget, Vygotsky, Goodman, Smith, Cambourne, and Halliday by creating a product that would "teach" the theory to novice learners. Working in small groups, they were to use both words and images to convey the information. Figure 11.5 outlines the assignment.

Figure 11.5
Language Development Project

You are to create and publish a picture book that demonstrates your understanding of one of the areas we have discussed during the section concerning language development. The audience for this picture book is your Phase I classmates. This is not a picture book for children. Your goal is to explain the theory to someone who is not familiar with the topic. You must provide all of the information so they will understand, using words and pictures. No specific length or format is required. Pictures may be original drawings, clip art, pages from magazines, or whatever source you may legally use. Possible topics include:

- Language Differences vs. Language Deficiencies
- Topic of your choice, (but be sure to obtain approval of the topic before you begin)
- Vygotsky's or Piaget's views of language and how it develops
- The Functions of Language—Halliday
- The Stages of Language Development—Smith, Meredith, and Goodman

• Conditions Under Which Children Learn to Talk—Brian Cambourne

To develop your understanding of the topic, use the articles you have been reading, information shared in class, learning from past classes, and/or other outside reading. If you feel the need to read more, I may be able to offer some suggestions.

You may work alone or with up to two other people.

Your finished book will be due _____.

You will be presenting it to the class on _____.

The rubric by which your book will be evaluated follows:

Students created picture books, big books, books with audio cassettes and video books to teach the information. Each project was very different in form and style. A rubric (see Figure 11.6) was given to each group before they began working describing how the project would be evaluated. Few guidelines were given to students about how they must do the project to avoid limiting their thinking. However, the rubric did provide some security, because students knew how the project would be evaluated.

Figure 11.6
Rubric—Language Development Project

20 points   Clarity of presentation of the concepts

_____1. The picture book clearly conveys an understanding of the topic.
_____2. The picture book conveys a surface understanding of the topic.
_____3. The picture book does not clearly convey an understanding of the topic.

20 points   Accuracy of the information

_____1. All of the information is accurately presented.
_____2. Most of the information is accurately presented.
_____3. Little of the information is accurately presented.

20 points Risk taking

_____　Vygotsky, Piaget, or Language Differences (20)
_____　Conditions　Favoring　Language　Development (Cambourne) (15)
_____　Stages of Language Development (Goodman et al.) or Functions of Language (Halliday) (10).
_____　Other (To be negotiated).
_____　Unrelated topic.

10 points Information presented both visually and in words

_____　Both images and words work together to bring about understanding of the material.
_____　Both words and images are used, but do not work together well to present a coherent message.
_____　Does not use both words and pictures.

10 Points Originality and creativity

_____　The picture book demonstrates evidence of thought and problem solving.
_____　The picture book demonstrates evidence of presenting the information in a very academic way.
_____　The picture book does not meet the requirements of the assignment.

10 points Quality of the product

_____　The mechanics and construction are of professional quality.
_____　The book contains some mechanical errors and/or the physical construction of the book is not of professional quality.
_____　The book contains many mechanical errors and/or the book is shabbily constructed.

10 points Completion of the Reflection on the Product Form

_____　The form is completed and shows evidence of productive reflection.
_____　The form is completed, but responses are only surface comments.
_____　　　The form is not completed.

_____/100　　Total points

Reflection on the Product Form

1. What is the best thing about your project?

2. Why do you like this feature?

3. What is the weakest feature of your project?

4. If you had two more weeks to complete this project, what would you have done differently?

5. How well do you understand the concepts you described in this project?

6. How much effort did you put into the completion of this project?

Conclusion

Collaboration offers so many opportunities to maximize learning. By expanding the view of assessment/evaluation to include more than paper/pencil activities, assessment and evaluation procedures can actually be a part of the learning process. As collaborative groups evaluate both the processes and products that they have created and used, they enhance numerous skills. When students collaboratively evaluate their own exam, they are reviewing the information one more time to increase their understanding of the concepts and relationships. As they communicate about the evaluation process, they improve their collaborative and communication skills. Assessment and evaluation become opportunities to improve learning—the real purpose of the college classroom.

REFERENCES

Anthony, R. J., Johnson, T.D., Mickelson, N.I., & Prece, A. (1991). *Evaluating Literacy: A Perspective for Change*. Portsmouth, NH: Heinemann.

Herman, J. L., Aschbacher, P. R., & Winters, L. (1992). *A Practical Guide to Alternative Assessment*. Alexandria, VA: Association for Supervision and Curriculum Development.

Marzano, R. J., Pickering, D., & McTighe, J. (1993). *Assessing Student Outcomes*. Alexandria, VA: Association for Supervision and Curriculum Development.

Slavin, R. E. (1990). *Cooperative Learning: Theory, Research, and Practice*. Englewood Cliff, NJ: Prentice Hall.

PART IV
OFF TO A GOOD START

Getting off to a good start using collaborative learning is difficult to do with limited knowledge. This section provides enough information and techniques to help an instructor get started using collaborative learning as rapidly as possible. After getting started, the reader may turn to the rest of the book for more in-depth information and techniques.

Lawrence Lyman provides some background and activities that may be used prior to forming cooperative groups. Group building is necessary since students today differ so much, for example, by home location, age, racial and ethnic group, and academic background.

Teresa A. Mehring offers specific strategies that are useful in large lecture environments. The collaborative approaches that she suggests can be applied to almost any large group setting. She uses Think-Pair-Share, KWL, Numbered Heads Together, and Jigsaw II.

Barbara J. Millis, Frank T. Lyman, Jr., and Neil Davidson provide background, information, and practical thoughts on the following readily usable cooperative structures: Think-Pair-Share, Roundtable, The Three-Step Interview, Numbered Heads Together, Pairs-Check, and Send/Pass a Problem. They also explain two structures that promote critical thinking: Jigsaw and Dyadic Essay Confrontations (DEC).

Douglas C. Foyle experienced (as an undergraduate student) and used (as a graduate student) the typical approach to the discussion sections that follow large lecture presentations. His use of Think-Pair-Share indicates that this strategy would be very helpful for graduate students who are thrust into a teaching role without a great deal of teacher training or methods.

This editor believes that faculty members who are beginning to use collaborative student-teacher processes should start by using Think-Pair-Share. Student learning would be greatly enhanced by using this simple-to-understand and simple-to-use strategy that is supported by research related to Cooperative Learning and wait time. The other cooperative structures mentioned in this section will help instructors expand their repertoire of useful student-involving strategies.

12

GROUP BUILDING IN THE COLLEGE CLASSROOM

by Lawrence Lyman

"Too many students in America go to school in a traditional, lonely classroom where they are isolated from their peers and taught to learn in silence. Too often, spontaneity and student interaction are punished rather than rewarded."
— Lawrence Lyman and Harvey C. Foyle (1990)

The examples of successful Cooperative Learning provided in this book attest to the benefits of promoting cooperative interaction among students in higher education classrooms. Unfortunately, the outcomes of implementing interactive strategies are often disappointing to instructors who do not begin their classes with activities designed to build group cohesion that will encourage students to work together cooperatively and share ideas with each other. A cohesive group shares a common mission and has the necessary skills and motivation to collaborate with other students in the classroom. The appropriate and planned use of group-building activities helps to create the cohesive atmosphere that is essential for cooperation, sharing, and collaboration.

Many college students are accustomed to remaining isolated from their peers and are reluctant to share ideas, preferring to let a few highly motivated students respond during class discussions. Previous experiences in high school and college classes have often demonstrated to students that many instructors expect minimal interaction among students.

Students frequently come to the college classroom from classrooms where content was presented in a rigid manner by the instructor with little invitation or opportunity for critical or creative thinking about that content with others. These experiences leave students ill-prepared for successful interaction in Cooperative Learning activities. Group-building activities provide opportunities for students to become accustomed to new expectations and to learn the benefits of interacting with other students.

Purposes of Group-Building Activities

Group-building activities can serve four important purposes. Group-building activities that allow students to become acquainted with each other can build a positive sense of classroom community. By using such activities, the instructor demonstrates his or her commitment to promoting student interaction and participation in the classroom. This sense of community can encourage students to interact more positively with each other and, according to some instructors, can increase student motivation and improve attendance.

Group-building activities also provide opportunities for the instructor to observe student interaction and to analyze the strengths and weaknesses of individuals. This data is important in structuring productive groups for further cooperation.

Group-building activities can also be used to focus the class on topics to be studied in class and to provide an anticipatory set for the learning to come. When such activities are used at the beginning of the class, the instructor is able to take attendance, return papers, or perform other needed duties while the students are actively engaged. Such group-building activities provide a transition between classroom topics and provide a needed break during longer classes.

Group-building activities can establish opportunities for critical and creative thinking. Many college students are reluctant to employ thinking skills, preferring instead to regurgitate material back to the instructor in the same manner in which it was learned. For long-term learning to take place, students must have opportunities to analyze, apply, and evaluate the material they are studying. In addition, group-building activities offer chances for students to think creatively about course content.

Components of Group-Building Activities

There are five essential components of a group-building activity, which are similar to the components of any well-planned Cooperative Learning activity, according to Lyman and Foyle (1990). First, students must work in heterogeneous groups, formed by the instructor, of students whose experiences, cultures, genders, and levels of achievement are different. By working with others who have different backgrounds, the student begins to appreciate his or her own strengths, as well as the strengths of others. Diversity in the classroom becomes an asset rather than a liability.

Second, group-building activities must be structured so that there is positive interdependence in the group. The individuals working together must have reason to do so. This component can be facilitated by providing only one set of materials for a group, structuring the activity so that it would be unlikely that any one student would know all the answers, or structuring the activity so that all must participate to complete the activity.

A third component of successful group-building activities is group reward. The group must be rewarded in some way for its work together. For K-12 students, a group reward may take the form of a bonus given to each member of the group, such as extra time at the computer or an additional pass to the library. For higher education students, a group reward may be recognition for the groups who have done a good job in group-building activities.

Group reward is often the fun inherent in a group-building activity. Activities that encourage creative thinking and problem solving in fun ways can stimulate student interest and cooperation without the need for additional reward. Grading of the group is almost always inappropriate during group-building activities, as individuals are just getting acquainted with one another and may be unskilled in cooperating.

Individual accountability is the fourth component of a successful group-building activity. Individuals in the group must be held accountable for their participation in the group.

This includes both individual effort to help the group accomplish its task and appropriate social interaction with others in the group, which may include listening, disagreeing constructively with other group members, or encouraging others in the group.

Individual accountability in group-building activities can be encouraged by the instructor as he or she interacts with the groups as they are working and provides positive feedback to individuals who are being helpful in the group. At the end of a group activity, group processing by the students may include feedback from group members to each other about how they feel each member helped the group complete the task. Students should be encouraged to keep their feedback positive.

Fifth, group-building activities must provide the groups with feelings of success. It is important to structure group-building activities so that all groups can do well if they put forth effort. Coercive aspects of activities, such as grading the groups should be removed because they may cause unnecessary anxiety and make it more difficult for group members to work together.

Building a Classroom Community

If students are to interact successfully in small-group discussions, study groups, laboratory teams, research teams, and other small-group cooperative structures, it is essential that the instructor provide opportunities for students to become acquainted with each other and to view classmates as friends and colleagues. It is especially important to model expectations for student involvement and interaction in teacher education courses so that future teachers will see the benefits of student interaction and encourage interaction and involvement in their own classes. Group-building activities are ideal for these purposes, particularly at the beginning of the class.

One strategy for helping students to get acquainted is to create a scavenger hunt activity using information that the students share with one another. During the initial class meeting, the instructor asks each student to write on an index card two unusual or interesting things about himself or herself. The student should be willing to share this information with other class members. The card also contains basic information about the student such as address, goals for the course, and previous course work related to the course.

The instructor selects one description for each student and prepares a sheet for the students to fill out. Figure 12.1 shows examples of descriptions shared in an undergraduate elementary education methods class.

Figure 12.1
Scavenger Hunt Descriptions

_____ played in a football game in the former Soviet Union.

_____ is a mother of three children who likes to ride motorcycles.

_____ has a grandmother who taught with the instructor in an elementary school.

_____ is the youngest of 10 children and has 25 nieces and nephews.

_____ works in the Financial Aid office on campus.

_____ is also earning a major in physical education.

_____ is captain of the university flag team.

_____ has a pet hamster named Hanna.

_____ plays four different musical instruments.

_____ likes to play softball, hunt, and fish.

_____ has three other family members born on her birthday.

_____ is a twin.

During the next class session, give each student a copy of the sheet and have them try to get each line signed by the correct classmate. This activity usually takes about 10 minutes.

For a similar activity, provide students with a sheet of general characteristics that may apply to many of your students. The items in Figure 12.2 were prepared for a graduate-level

Figure 12.2
Find a Person Who...

Directions: Find a person in this room who can sign each item. You must have a different signature for each line. The instructor will not sign any item.

_____   comes from a family of four or more children.

_____   has lived in a city with a population of 300,000 people or more.

_____   attended a private elementary school or high school.

_____   had fewer than 50 classmates in his or her high school graduating class.

_____   has traveled outside the United States.

_____   can tell you a joke that does not make fun of any individual or group of people.

_____   knows the name of the current U. S. Secretary of Education.

_____   knows how to program a VCR.

_____   knows the day of the week and the date when students will begin school this fall in his or her district.

_____   knows a child who has been abused or neglected.

_____   has worked in a fast-food restaurant at some time in his or her life.

_____   has read to a child or a group of children in the past week.

_____   can speak a language other than English.

_____   has been a member of a sports team since leaving college.

_____   has written a letter to a newspaper, legislator, governor, or the President in the past year.

class in instructional improvement. Each item can be related to a trend or issue of importance to educational change.

In the scavenger hunt group-building activities, all students must actively participate and interact with each other to promote positive interdependence. Each student is held accountable because each student has an individual sheet to complete. Most students find this type of activity enjoyable, and that, in turn, provides a group reward for working together. Because every student is involved, virtually every student can feel successful if he or she put forth effort to do the activity.

Activities that build classroom community involve individuals working together. These activities provide practice for further group interaction and provide opportunities for the instructor to analyze individual strengths and weaknesses.

In the following group-building activity (see Figure 12.3), students begin in pairs. For students who have had little experience with collaboration in previous classes, the pair structure is usually the easiest for beginning the process of learning to cooperate with others.

Observing Student Interaction

As the students are working in group-building activities that help to build a classroom community, the instructor should be observing the groups to gather data that will be useful in structuring further group-building activities and cooperative projects. The following list contains general guidelines for observation:

1. Which students are leaders in their groups?
2. Which students are shy or reticent in the group?
3. Which students do not get along well with other students?
4. Which students are skilled at getting along with others?
5. Which students have difficulty communicating in the group?
6. Which students have good verbal skills?
7. Which students appear to be well organized?
8. Which students appear to have good listening skills?

Figure 12.3
Matching Games

Objective: Students will work in pairs to identify common answers to given statements.

Procedure: Each pair of students is given a copy of the statements sheet. Ten minutes is usually appropriate for the students to write one response that they agree on for each of the twelve given items. After the pairs have finished, two pairs can be grouped together to stimulate additional discussion.

Statements Sheet

Something we like to do on Saturday mornings	Something we would buy if someone gave us each $1,000	Something we like to eat for a snack	A television show we watch
A famous person we would like to meet	Something that would make school better	A holiday that we wish would come more often	A color we like
Something we have in our rooms at home	One thing that we wish would happen at school this year	The most important thing a good friend does	One thing that would make this class a great place to be

Group Processing: After the groups of four have finished the task, have each group share their response to some of the items. The items "something that would make school better" and "one thing that would make this class a great place to be" can help the instructor set goals for class cooperation.

9. Which students appear to have a good academic or experiential background for the course?

By identifying these student characteristics as students work together in group-building activities, the teacher can better select heterogeneous groupings for other cooperative activities that will be likely to be productive.

Focusing and Setting the Class

The first minutes of the college class period can often be lost as students arrive late from distant points of the campus and the instructor completes routine tasks such as passing back papers or taking the roll. These first few minutes are the opportune time to focus the students' attention on the topic of the day through a group-building activity.

In the group builder in Figure 12.4, students are encouraged to think of both sides of a question instead of simply agreeing or disagreeing. This group builder was used in a graduate level class before a discussion of conflict management takes place.

The activity in Figure 12.5 serves as a set for small-group discussion about the effect of home environment on student readiness for school and success in school.

Figure 12.4
Seeing Both Sides

Objective: Students will give examples to support agreement and disagreement with a given saying.

Procedure: Students are placed in heterogeneous groups. Each group is given a saying. (These may be selected at random by group members selecting a piece of paper with a saying on it from a hat or other container.)

The following instructions are printed on the chalkboard or on an overhead transparency:

1. As a group, agree on what you think your saying means.
2. As a group, think of one situation where the saying would be correct.
3. As a group, think of one situation where the saying would not be correct.
4. Choose someone who is willing to share your group's ideas with the whole group when the instructor calls on your group.

Example:
The saying is:"The shortest distance between two points is a straight line."

One situation where the saying would be correct: When there is a highway or road between two places.

One situation where the saying would be incorrect: When there is a mountain in between the two places and it is faster to go around than over it.

Possible sayings to use:
1. Honesty is the best policy.
2. No pain, no gain.
3. Two heads are better than one.
4. Nice people finish last.
5. A penny saved is a penny earned.
6. You can't judge a book by its cover.
7. The more, the merrier.
8. Children should be seen and not heard.
9. Early to bed, early to rise, makes a person healthy, wealthy, and wise.
10. It is better to give than to receive.

Group processing: Each group shares its ideas with the class.

The activity in Figure 12.5 serves as a set for small-group discussion about the effect of home environment on student readiness for school and success in school.

Figure 12.5
House or Home?

Objective: Students will identify references to "house" and "home" from a variety of sources.

Procedure: Students are grouped in heterogeneous groups. Each group is given a copy of the reference sheet referring to"house" or "home." The groups are instructed to think of the house or home that would fit each description. For example, a high school class would be "home economics."

1. where the deer and the antelope play
2. it's been the ruin of many a poor boy in New Orleans
3. where ghosts and goblins live
4. the city you come from
5. this coffee is good to the last drop
6. fraternity movie starring John Belushi
7. this bird is trained to come back
8. if you live in one, don't throw stones
9. not store bought
10. 1600 Pennsylvania Avenue
11. where plants and flowers grow
12. movie where a boy frustrates burglars by himself
13. beats two pair in poker
14. where you are if you're in trouble
15. where your Congressman or Congresswoman works
16. an annoying insect you try to swat
17. wrote *The Iliad* and *The Odyssey*
18. where The Star-Spangled Banner still waves
19. chocolate chip cookies
20. Hank Aaron hit the most

Answers: (1) Home on the Range, (2) The House of the Rising Sun, (3) haunted house, (4) home town, (5) Maxwell House, (6) Animal House, (7) homing pigeon, (8) glass house, (9) home-made, (10) the White House, (11) greenhouse, (12) Home Alone, (13) full house, (14) the dog house, (15) House of Representatives, (16) house fly, (17) Homer, (18) the home of the brave, (19) toll house, (20) home runs

Group processing: After answers are shared, the instructor asks groups to discuss how much effect the home environment of a student has on his or her success in school.

Encouraging Critical Thinking

Critical and creative thinking may be encouraged with group-building activities that support the application, analysis, and evaluation of ideas. Higher-level thinking should occur when groups are given short tasks that require problem solving, analytical skills, or research skills, especially when they are encouraged to work as a group to determine solutions. The desired product can sometimes be obtained or enhanced by using research materials.

The examples provided in this section are generic but can be easily adapted to specific course content. In the activity in Figure 12.6, students are asked to think of past or present famous persons who might have made the given understatements. While several responses could be possible for some of the examples, many groups will tend to think of the same answers. The instructor may want to recognize unique answers generated by groups for given statements.

Creative thinking is facilitated through group-building activities that provide opportunities for brainstorming, creativity, and synthesis. When students work together, they are likely to take risks more frequently during the creative process and are often more likely to be willing to share their responses with other students.

In the activity in Figure 12.7, students are asked to brainstorm creative responses. Brainstorming may be difficult for some college students, because they are required to generate many possible answers instead of focusing on a single answer.

Instructors should remind students that during the brainstorming process all responses are acceptable because ideas are being collected and that responses can be evaluated after the group runs out of ideas. Brainstorming can be assessed by determining teams with the greatest number of responses or by identifying teams with answers not thought of by other teams.

Figure 12.6
Understatement

Objective: Students will identify celebrities who meet given criteria.

Procedure: Students are grouped in heterogeneous groups. A list of the following understatements is written on the chalkboard, presented on an overhead transparency or provided on paper for each group. The instructor explains that these statements are understatements that real or fictional famous persons might have made. An example might be "I was a little taller than most." An appropriate response would be Paul Bunyan. The instructor should emphasize that several correct answers may be possible for each understatement.

1. We had a little rain lately.
2. I can play basketball a little.
3. I guess I did invent a thing or two.
4. I do some writing now and then.
5. You can see me in a commercial every once in awhile.
6. I get into a little trouble from time to time.
7. A few people were a tiny bit concerned about my honesty.
8. I am a pretty good tennis player for someone my age.
9. I didn't do very well in the war.
10. I might have gotten sort of lost.

Answers (others are possible): (1) Noah, (2) Shaquille O'Neal, Charles Barkley, (3) Thomas Edison, Benjamin Franklin, (4) Stephen King, Mary Higgins Clark, (5) Michael Jordan, Bill Cosby, (6) Dennis the Menace, (7) Richard Nixon, (8) Jimmy Connors, (9) Saddam Hussein, (10) Christopher Columbus

Group Processing: Students can generate additional examples of understatements that might relate to schools. For example: "That group is a little hard to handle" (for the worst class ever) or "That bus driver made a little mistake" (for a bus driver who took students to the wrong school).

Figure 12.7
Bigger Than a Bread Box

Objective: Students will brainstorm things that begin with the letter *B* that are larger than a bread box.

Procedure: Students are placed in heterogeneous groups. The team appoints one member to write ideas for the team. Teams are advised that dictionaries and other research sources may not be used during this activity. Students are instructed to think of as many things as they can that begin with *B* that are larger than a bread box. Students are given approximately 5-7 minutes to brainstorm.

Possible answers: 1. baby, 2. barrel, 3. basement, 4. Bill Clinton, 5. Brazil, 6. Buick, 7. building, 8. bull, 9. Butte, Montana

Group Processing: Students appoint one person from their group to share answers. The person cannot be the same one who wrote the answers. Group writers are instructed to let the reader know if their group had that answer written down, and all groups with the answer cross it off their list. All groups share any ideas that have not been crossed off. The groups with the most original ideas (not thought of by other groups) are recognized.

Conclusion

Because successful interaction with others is crucial to success in many occupational fields, in marriage and other social relationships, and in community service, college classrooms should provide opportunities for frequent collaboration among students. Group-building activities are usually necessary before other Cooperative Learning activities can be successful.

Group-building activities are effective in building a sense of community to encourage productive learning. Group-building activities provide opportunities for the instructor to analyze student strengths and weaknesses and to make appropriate groupings for later cooperative activities. Group-building activities are used to focus or set the class, to practice critical thinking, and to encourage creative thinking.

RESOURCE MATERIALS

The Encyclopedia of Icebreakers. (1983). San Diego, CA: University Associates Inc.

Johnson, R., & Johnson, D. (1985). *Cooperative Learning: Warm-ups, Grouping Strategies, and Group Activities*. Edina, MN: Interaction Book Company.

Maeroff, G. I. (1993). *Team Building for School Change: Equipping Teachers for New Roles*. New York: Teachers College Press.

Scannel, E. E., & Newstrom, J. W. (1991). *Still More Games Trainers Play: Experiential Learning Exercises*. New York: McGraw-Hill, Inc.

Slavin, R. E. (1990). *Cooperative Learning: Theory, Research, and Practice*. Englewood Cliffs, NJ: Prentice Hall.

REFERENCE

Lyman, L., & Foyle, H. C. (1990). *Cooperative Grouping for Interactive Learning: Students, Teachers, and Administrators*. Washington, DC: National Education Association.

13

COOPERATIVE LEARNING IN PSYCHOLOGY 370

by Teresa A. Mehring

The most popular instructional method in higher education, the lecture method, has been the target of criticism for several centuries. Critics have called it an anachronism; they've blamed it for imposing an undesirable passive role on students and for being nonadaptive to the individual student's needs. In traditional college classrooms, students have responsibility only for themselves, are not allowed to help one another, and must compete for grades. Cooperative Learning approaches to instruction can alter these conditions.

An additional concern with traditional college classrooms is the focus on goal structures that are individualistic and competitive. Many college faculty take great pride in announcing on the first day of class that 3 percent of the class will receive A's, 13 percent B's, 68 percent C's, 13 percent D's, and 3 percent F's. This scenario provides a classic illustration of a competitive goal structure. Other college classrooms foster the individualistic philosophy. Each student completes varied projects, quizzes, and papers. Then the student receives a grade based on individual performance. Cooperative Learning provides an alternative to these two goal structures. With Cooperative Learning, small groups of students (typically four to six students) work together on application or practice exercises.

Slavin (1989) defined Cooperative Learning as "a set of instructional methods in which students are encouraged or required to work together on academic tasks" (p. 6). He noted that such methods may include having students sit together for discussion, or help each other with assignments, and more complex requirements. Critical attributes of Cooperative Learning include the following: all students learn the same material, there is no tutor, and the initial information comes from the teacher.

Five basic elements need to be included for a lesson to be cooperative: positive interdependence, face-to-face interaction, individual accountability, collaborative skills, and group processing (Johnson & Johnson, 1989). Dembo (1991) elaborated on each of these elements:

> The first [element] is positive interdependence. The students must perceive that they "sink or swim" together. This means that they must share goals, divide the tasks, share resources, information, assume responsibility for different roles, and, most important, receive rewards based on their group performance.
>
> The second element requires face-to-face interaction among students so that they discuss the nature of the task, decide how they can best work together, and explain to each other how to solve problems. The importance of helping others is emphasized.
>
> The third element is individual accountability for learning the assigned material. Each student must develop a sense of personal responsibility to the group. A key to success in cooperative learning is for each member to master material so that he or she can help other members of the group achieve success.
>
> The fourth element is collaborative skills. Obviously, placing students in groups and telling them to work cooperatively without teaching them the necessary social skills will not lead to compatible working relationships within the group.
>
> The final element in cooperative learning is group processing, which occurs when groups discuss and evaluate their progress and maintain effective working relationships among members. (pp. 346-347)

There are numerous models for organizing cooperative learning in classrooms. Johnson and Johnson (1986) advocate the "conceptual approach." This approach espouses the five critical characteristics just described.

Slavin (1983) proposed the "curriculum approach." This model includes four key curriculum packages: Team Accelerated Instruction (TAI), Cooperative Integrated Reading & Composition (CIRC); Teams-Games-Tournaments (TGT); and Student Teams-Achievement Divisions (STAD). Each of these four curriculum packages focuses on cooperative learning and basic skill instruction.

A third model, The Structural Approach, has been described by Kagan (1993). This approach is based on the creation, analysis, and application of content-free structures that cause students to interact in positive ways in the class-room. Content-free structures, usable with any content, enable an instructor to make multiple applications of a single struc-ture within a variety of subjects. Kagan's structures fall into three groups: In Turn, Jigsaw, and Match-Ups.

A fourth model, The Group Investigation Approach (Sharan & Sharan, 1976), combines the conceptual and struc-tural approaches. Students work together to plan how they will find answers to key questions about a topic of mutual interest. The group breaks down the work into individual or pair investigation tasks. Each person gathers the assigned information and brings it to the group for discussion, synthe-sis, and reporting to the class. The teacher plays the major facilitating role through each stage of this inquiry process.

A fifth, and final model, is called The IRI Synthesis Approach (Bellanca & Fogarty, 1991). This model synthesizes effective elements from the other five models with best prac-tices on thinking skills, metacognition, cognitive organizers, and learning for transfer. This model uses the acronym BUILD as an organizational schema—(Build in higher-order thinking for transfer; Unite teams in face-to-face interaction; Insure individual learning; Look over and discuss the interaction; Develop social skills of cooperation for life (p. 252).

The purpose of this chapter is to describe how four different Cooperative Learning structures have been incorpo-rated into an upper level, undergraduate, psychology course—PY 370, Psychology of the Mentally Retarded. The class size generally averages between 60 and 70 students. Most students are juniors or seniors majoring in psychology, special education, elementary education, or vocational reha-bilitation. The four structures—Thing-Pair-Square, KWL, Numbered Heads Together, and Jigsaw—have been used rou-tinely each semester for the past three years.

Think-Pair-Square

This Cooperative Learning structure (a form of Think-Pair-Share that has an additional step in which the pair shares with another pair) is used at the beginning of each class session as a review activity. A question is posed (e.g., describe the eugenics movement), students think alone for a brief period of time (one to two minutes), then form pairs to discuss the question with someone sitting nearby. Once pairs have finished sharing, the pair combines with a new pair to discuss the question. Two or three students are generally called upon to share answers, allowing the professor to reinforce or elaborate on the answers given. Then the professor usually poses three to four review questions covering material introduced during the previous class session.

In addition to its application as a review strategy, Think-Pair-Square can also be used in the following ways:

- after a lecture, to help students summarize key points,
- to begin a new topic or unit by having students discuss prior knowledge,
- to stimulate student thinking about important information,
- to check students' understanding of or insight into a topic,
- to bring closure to a class session,
- to deepen students' short-term memories, or
- to promote student transfer of a concept.

What We Know (KWL)

KWL is a cognitive rehearsal strategy used to diagnose prior knowledge students possess about a topic. Since the PY 370 class is an upper division course, students have already completed PY 100 Introduction to Psychology and PY 211 Developmental Psychology. KWL is used to determine what students already know about selected topics that have been presented in lower division courses (e.g., intelligence, Piaget's stages of cognitive development). Teams of four are provided a large sheet of butcher paper (approximately 3 feet x 4 feet) and asked to divide the paper into three columns:

What We Know	What We Want to Know	What We Learned

Teams brainstorm and record what they already know about the topic in the first column. Next, they brainstorm and record what they want to know about the topic. After a specified time limit (usually about 20 minutes), each team shares their list with another team. A representative from each team then shares items from the What We Know and What We Want to Know columns with the entire class.

This approach allows the instructor to tailor information presented in class to the needs of the class. Instead of using valuable time giving a watered-down, global overview of a topic, the instructor can provide in-depth information on selected aspects of a topic, while enriching and expanding upon topics about which students already possess a good grasp of salient knowledge.

Once learning activities related to the topic are completed, teams reunite to discuss and record What Has Been Learned in the third column. The concepts listed in the third column provide an excellent means of self-assessment for the instructor. If the majority of teams list a topic as something that was learned, the instructor can feel confident that this information was well presented. If an essential concept is listed by few teams, it is a clear message that this concept needs to be retaught. It may also be a cue to the instructor that alternative presentation styles need to be considered in future courses. A sample (abbreviated) KWL chart from a four-member Cooperative Learning group is presented in Figure 13.1.

Figure 13.1
Sample KWL Chart for Unit on Intelligence

What We Know	What We Want to Know	What We Learned
Psychologists have developed tests for intelligence.	Are I.Q. tests accurate/reliable?	Four major theories about intelligence.
It can be improved or increased through education.	Is there any way to measure intelligence besides I.Q. tests?	Effects of heredity and environment.
Different people have different levels of intelligence.	Does intelligence stay constant throughout the life span?	Overview of Stanford Binet IV and WISC-III.
Many factors influence intelligence.	How much do heredity and environment affect intelligence?	How I.Q. tests are used to place special education labels on children.
There are two categories of intelligence: fluid and crystallized.	How do different areas of the brain affect intelligence? How do drugs affect intelligence?	Social I.Q. is not tested but is important.

Numbered Heads Together

This simple four-step procedure is used as a review process prior to the midterm and final examinations. In Step 1, students number off so that each student is assigned a number: 1, 2, 3, or 4. In Step 2, the instructor asks each group to make sure that every member can answer a question that generally involves multiple responses and higher-level thinking skills (e.g., Which gender is affected by sex-linked genetic traits and why?). In Step 3, four-member teams "put their heads together" and discuss the correct answer. In Step 4, the instructor calls a number (1, 2, 3, or 4), and students on each team who have that number who know the answer either stand or raise their hands to respond. Either an individual student is asked to share the answer with the rest of the class or all students with the specified number are asked to state an answer if it can be provided using key words or phrases using a choral response format. If, for example, only three of a possible twelve students who are number one's indicate that they know the answer, teams are asked to put their heads together again until more number one's know the correct response. If, after a few minutes, more number one's don't indicate that they know the response, the instructor should take the opportunity to review or reteach the concept.

The Numbered Heads Together structure includes all of the elements of Cooperative Learning teams: a management system, motivation and ability for students to cooperate, positive interdependence, individual accountability, and simultaneous interaction. It is also an activity that students enjoy. Most students benefit directly from the activity through improved scores on the midterm and final examinations.

Jigsaw II

There are many forms of Jigsaw that can be used in a variety of ways for a variety of goals. Jigsaw's main purpose (See Aronson, 1980) is to have each team member become responsible for a specific piece of learning, and then to share that piece with teammates. Slavin (1980) described a variation of Jigsaw called Jigsaw II. It is this variation that is used in PY 370 as a means for students to cover textbook chapters or other assigned readings that require little or no elaboration from the instructor.

Step 1: Form cooperative teams. Students number off so that each student is a 1, 2, 3, 4, 5, or 6.

Step 2: Form "expert groups." Each number 1 meets with number 1's from all other teams. Number 2's meet with 2's, and so on. Each expert group is assigned a specific topic from the chapter or assigned reading. Once each member within the expert group has read the material, expert group members discuss the topic, pinpointing salient information. (Sometimes discussion questions are provided to assist the expert group in focusing on critical information.) Each expert group designs a mnemonic, flow chart, visual illustration, or some other strategy that each group member will use to share information from the assigned reading with cooperative team members. The instructor circulates among each expert group as the instructional strategy is being designed to ensure accuracy and thoroughness of the content.

Step 3: Experts present reports and take a quiz. Students return to a cooperative team that has a 1, 2, 3, 4, 5, and 6. Each student reports what was learned within the respective expert groups. To ensure that all students possess critical information, the instructor may pose ten to fifteen single-word or short-phrase questions, asking the class to respond using choral response. Generally, a quiz is administered during the next class period. Students receive an individual quiz score and a team quiz score. The individual score is the total number of correct responses. A team score is determined by adding one point to each individual score if every member of the cooperative team responds correctly to a question. Figure 13.2 is an illustration of Jigsaw II.

Figure 13.2
Jigsaw II Illustration

Step 1: Cooperative teams are formed.

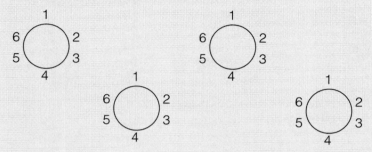

Step 2: Expert groups discuss assigned reading.

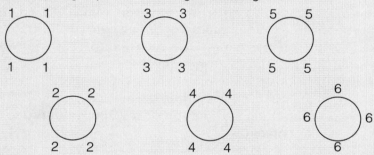

Step 3: Experts report to cooperative groups.

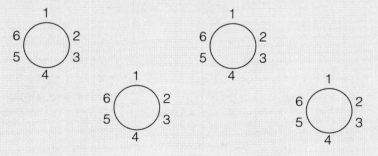

Benefits

The Cooperative Learning structures described in this chapter have resulted in several beneficial outcomes:

1. Students were more responsible for their own learning.
2. Students learned to value and respect opinions and contributions of classmates, including those expressed by international students and students from varied ethnic and cultural backgrounds.
3. Performance on quizzes and examinations improved, and students demonstrated increased levels of understanding of the course content.
4. Students from diverse majors (elementary and secondary education, psychology, vocational rehabilitation, and special education) had the opportunity to explore topics drawing upon the perspectives of varied disciplines of study.
5. Students enjoyed coming to class!

Challenges

Implementing Cooperative Learning in the college classroom poses several unique challenges to the instructor:

1. Many college classes are large—40, 50, or more students. Often the seating arrangements are not conducive to group interaction. This can be overcome by having students branch out into an additional classroom, going outdoors, or scattering to various corners of a large lecture hall.
2. International students may lack the verbal fluency in English to communicate easily with peers. Pairing the international student with a buddy or having instructor meetings with the student to ensure knowledge of critical information prior to participation in cooperative teams, may minimize potential difficulty.

3. The instructor must plan Cooperative Learning activities prior to implementation. The instructor must plan for how cooperative groups will be assigned (by numbering off or by gender, discipline, birthdates, or some other variable); provide appropriate materials (butcher paper and markers, or assigned readings); and make arrangements for additional classrooms if needed.
4. Some students have had minimal experience or preparation for group learning. Simply placing students in groups does not result in increased learning for all students. Group interaction skills need to be reviewed and/or taught.

Conclusion

The type and amount of Cooperative Learning that a college professor adopts is partially a function of what the instructor sees as the goal of teaching. Some faculty members value individual performance and competitiveness; others value cooperation. Ideally, the college classroom should provide as broad a range of learning experiences to students as possible, including a variety of structured and unstructured Cooperative Learning experiences, and a balance of competitive and individualistic learning experiences. Such opportunities will better prepare students to function well across the whole range of life's challenges.

REFERENCES

Aronson, E. (1980). "Training Teachers to Use Jigsaw Learning: A Manual for Teachers." In S. Sharan, P. Hare, C. D. Webb, B. R. Hertz-Lazarowitz, eds. *Cooperation in Education*. Provo, UT: Brigham Young Press.

Bellanca, J., & Fogarty, R. (1991). *Blueprints for Thinking in the Cooperative Classroom*. Palatine, IL: Skylight Publishing.

Dembo, M. H. (1991). *Applying Educational Psychology in the Classroom*. 14th ed. New York: Longman Publishing Company.

Johnson, D.W., & Johnson, R. (1986). *Circles of Learning in the Classroom*. Alexandria, VA: Association for Supervision and Curriculum Development.

————. (1989). *Cooperation and Competition: Theory and Research*. Edina, MN: Interaction Book Company.

Kagan, S. (1993). *Cooperative Learning*. San Juan Capistrano, CA: Kagan Cooperative Learning.

Sharan, S., & Sharan, Y. (1976). *Small-Group Teaching*. Englewood Cliffs, NJ: Educational Technology Publications.

Slavin, R. (1980). *Using Student Team Learning*. rev. ed. Baltimore, MD: The Center for Social Organization of Schools, The Johns Hopkins University.

————. (1983). *Cooperative Learning*. New York: Longman.

————. (1989). *Cooperative Learning: Theory, Research, and Practice*. Englewood Cliffs, NJ: Prentice-Hall.

14

COOPERATIVE STRUCTURES FOR HIGHER EDUCATION CLASSROOMS

by Barbara Millis, Frank T. Lyman, Jr., and
Neil Davidson

Higher education remains ever fluid. Quality and accountability issues and the resulting scrutiny of faculty roles and rewards—how and why professors spend their time— have prompted faculty to reexamine some of their basic academic premises. This reflection has been stimulated by additional forces such as the assessment movement; the necessity for life-long learning in a technologically driven, multicultural workplace; the influx of nontraditional students, including minorities, international students, and part-time working adults; and an increasing awareness that time-worn methods of delivery such as unrelieved reliance on the lecture no longer work for a majority of students.

Good lectures, of course, are valuable, but most faculty members continue to use only this approach and a basic lecture/recitation format, in which the professor speaks, asks questions, and a few students answer or comment. This seemingly intractable paradigm is at best a combination of TV's *Jeopardy* and public speaking, and at worst a tyranny of extroverts competing for scarce talk time. As a marketplace of ideas and a training ground for thinking, the university setting should encourage a maximum number of students to participate and to contribute.

For many reasons, an increasing number of faculty members are turning to Cooperative Learning, a structured form of group work where students who are individually assessed work toward common group goals. Smith, Johnson, and Johnson (1992), after a review of the Cooperative Learning research, note these four trends:

1. Interest in Cooperative Learning in colleges and universities is growing at an incredible rate.
2. Cooperative Learning is equally or more effective than lecturing in helping student(s) master conceptual material and in helping them develop cooperative skills.
3. Cooperative Learning is being implemented in a wide range of courses and programs including health sciences, law, engineering, math and science, writing, communication, study skills, professional development, and teacher preparation.
4. Instructors are applying Cooperative Learning in a variety of ways—cooperative lecture, base groups, formal task groups, structured controversy discussion groups, jigsaw groups, and computer enhanced courses. (pp. 34-35)

Slavin (1993), another important Cooperative Learning researcher, contends that "After many years in elementary and secondary schools, Cooperative Learning (CL) is finally going to college. Of course, CL has long existed in post-secondary education; study groups, discussion groups, and work groups of various kinds are hardly new. . . . What is new in recent years is that post-secondary professors are beginning to use CL as a major focus of their teaching, and research on such applications in higher education is growing. This is an important and fundamental change" (p. 2).

Research-oriented higher education faculty members may be swayed by the endorsement of Cooperative Learning in Astin's (1993) comprehensive longitudinal study of the impact of college on undergraduate students. Using samples from 159 baccalaureate granting institutions, Astin investigated 22 outcomes affected by 88 environmental factors to determine influences on students' academic achievement, personal development, and satisfaction with college. He determined that two factors in particular, student-student interaction and student-faculty interaction, carried the largest weights and affected the largest number of general education outcomes. Because of the influence of peers and faculty, he concludes that "How students approach general education (and how the faculty actually deliver the curriculum) is far more important than the formal curricular content and structure" (p. 425). He unequivocally endorses Cooperative Learning as a valid and effective pedagogical approach:

> Under what we have come to call cooperative learning methods, where students work together in small groups, students basically teach each other, and our pedagogical resources are multiplied. Classroom research has consistently shown that cooperative learning approaches produce outcomes that are superior to those obtained through traditional competitive approaches, and it may well be that our findings concerning the power of the peer group offer a possible explanation: cooperative learning may be more potent than traditional methods of pedagogy because it motivates students to become more active and more involved participants in the learning process. This greater involvement could come in at least two different ways. First, students may be motivated to expend more effort if they know their work is going to be scrutinized by peers; and second, students may learn course material in greater depth if they are involved in helping teach it to fellow students. (p. 427)

The research base for Cooperative Learning is complemented by a theoretical framework predicated on a belief in the potential of all students to succeed. Furthermore, Cooperative Learning is based on a constructivist view of knowledge, one in which students come to know something by building on existing schemata, constantly testing, revising, and refining knowledge within a social setting. The research and theoretical bases for Cooperative Learning are important for faculty members because they give the "why" behind the "what." But because of Cooperative Learning's relatively wide acceptance in academia, increasingly faculty are asking "how?" They want practical implementation strategies.

Classroom management issues need to be addressed as they do for any practitioners. Faculty members want to know how to form groups and how long to keep students together: They need to understand monitoring processes: Evaluation is a key concern: They are also worried about potential problems such as dysfunctional groups. The Cooperative Learning literature provides answers to these questions, and colleagues—particularly those in similar disciplines—can offer practical advice. But probably the most important appeal of Cooperative Learning lies in the fact that the theory can be put into practive by using specific structures. Structures are essentially content-free procedures that can be used in virtually any discipline for a variety of purposes. When content is added to a structure it becomes a specific classroom activity. When a series of activities are linked, they become a lesson or unit plan. Faculty members who become familiar with these structures, usually through interactive workshops, reading, or discussions with colleagues, suddenly understand the "how" and feel more confident about initiating Cooperative Learning in their own classrooms. Probably the easiest structure to initiate is Think-Pair-Share.

Think-Pair-Share and Variations

Think-Pair-Share (Lyman, 1992) offers hope for a paradigm shift to a more responsive higher education classroom. In this structure, students always think for three seconds or more, sometimes have interaction with partners, and sometimes discuss issues with the entire class. Combined with other variables such as intrinsic motivation, responsive writing, additional structures that encourage academic interactions, and a disposition toward metacognition, this structured Cooperative Learning technique can create a climate for student attentiveness and response.

Although the Think-Pair-Share technique, as such, originated in the elementary schools, variations of it are used in secondary and higher education classrooms. The following college-level scenarios should provide a basis for an understanding of the implementation and effectiveness of Think-Pair-Share.

In a college physics class, the professor provides a visual model with two possible exit trajectories for an object moving rapidly through a concentrically curved tube. He asks the students to take three minutes to predict the path by drawing it on paper and to derive and write down the governing principle of force (think). After three minutes, and upon a cue for pair talk, the students attempt to come to a consensus with a preselected partner (pair). After two minutes of pair discussion, during which the professor circulates to observe, a spokesperson for each pair indicates by a hand signal which path the pair predicted (share). At this juncture, the professor has several options, using the next level of Think-Pair-Share. If most of the students have the correct answer, the professor could have each pair discuss the principle with another pair (Think-Pair-Square), but since the majority of the pairs have the other answer, the professor repeats the basic pattern. Thus, he or she asks the students to derive the principle for the correct answer independently (think), discuss it in pairs (pair), and then elaborate on the principles as a whole class discussion (share).

The above scenario contains the essential elements of Think-Pair-Share: independent thinking, structured pair cooperative talk, and large group discussion. Think-Pair-Share is the vehicle that allows all students to participate in high-level concrete to abstract thinking.

As another example, in an undergraduate class on learning theory, the professor poses the question: "How do people learn?" Independently, students use a list of examples of learning to derive a set of causal factors, which they place on a web-shaped visual diagram, or visual organizer. After five minutes, the professor instructs the students to talk with partners and justify their choices by giving examples. Next, students return to the independent think mode, place the learning factors (such as imitation or association) in the inside ring segments of a concentric circle visual organizer, and write supporting examples (such as baby talk or mnemonics) in the concentric ring. The professor then signals for the class to share and ascertains with the students which causal factors are most common. Finally, he or she hands out a set of research-based theoretical learning factors and asks the students to find similarities between the factors on their wheels and the theoretical set of factors. At the end of class, the professor collects the students' concentrically ordered wheels in order to fashion a large template from all available knowledge.

This second scenario reveals the fit between Think-Pair-Share and a constructive theory-making/theory-matching

activity. Cognitive mapping, or diagramming in a visual organizer, is the generating and focusing element, and justifying is
the structure for pair talk, as was reaching consensus in the
first scenario. A third scenario will reveal other Think-Pair-
Share variations.

The study of nationalism focuses on causes and effects
of European public mood preceding World Wars I and II.
When the history students enter the class, they spend three
minutes writing what they remember about the public mood
from the prior day's lecture and reading. Upon a cue, they
exchange papers with a partner (they have a new partner
each class), read the papers, and from pair discussion, add in
writing whatever they can from the partner's recollection.
After four minutes of pair work, the professor begins a lecture
on the causes of nationalistic fervor in World War I. In ten
minutes, he or she stops the lecture and asks the students to
prepare to teach their partners the causes by using examples
from their prior knowledge, that is, by connecting cause(s)
with effects. In this case, the "teachers" alternate taking one
exemplified cause after another while the students add on to
what is taught. The professor then makes the connections in
another short lecture, and after six minutes asks the students
to connect, orally, any examples that he or she didn't men-
tion. The professor concludes by using a similar strategy for
World War II, and having the students independently make a
Venn (intersecting circles) diagram, to compare the public
moods before the two wars. Tomorrow they will attempt to
reach consensus on the Venn diagrams with a partner and justify their conclusions with another pair before the professor
gives his or her opinion.

This third scenario includes more Think-Pair-Share
structures. The bridging activity at the beginning and end of
the class creates continuity. Pair-add on, pair-alternate, and
pair-teach are three more pair structures. In directing students
to compare, to exemplify, and to connect cause and effect,
the professor uses a form of "metacognitive anchoring" to give
students direction on exactly how their minds are to function
as they think, thus preventing the "cognitive drift" that occurs
with vague prompts such as "find supporting details." Also,

students should feel empowered and more curious when their thinking precedes the lecture, as well as more attentive when they know they may have to, at any moment, think, write, and talk with a partner about the content.

A final scenario will illustrate the fit of Think-Pair-Share to the self-assessment and constructivist, or theory-making, aspects of learning. The English education professor's objective is to teach the teacher candidates to do quality descriptive writing and to recognize the quality. The professor reads five descriptive passages from great literature and has the students read the scenes independently. He then displays five scenic pictures and asks the students to pick one and make it come to life in writing. After they have written for ten minutes, the professor directs them to choose their three best descriptive phrases or sentences. He then has them switch papers with partners and ask the partners to bracket the three best descriptive phrases. The pairs then match and justify their choices to each other. The students write another description and repeat the evaluative process. After listening to descriptions, and then writing with pair evaluation several more times, the students derive individually, in pairs, and with another pair, a set of criteria for quality descriptive writing. They then compare this rubric to that of the professor, and go through the Think-Pair-Share cycle to create, as a class, a concentric circle diagram that connects each criterion to an example. The professor and students will use this theoretical design to assess descriptive writing. In not allowing the usual "rush to rubric," in which students are asked to derive criteria from limited examples, the professor emphasizes the efficacy of modeling and of student-constructed theory, thereby revealing to the students their own power to learn both the practice and theory of any process.

Think-Pair-Share is then a multifaceted cooperative technique, a vehicle for learning to learn as well as for learning. Students receive a positive message about their own cognitive and social competency when they bring a thought-out response to a cooperative discourse in which everyone has had a chance to respond. The ingredients of structured, independent think-time and pair-interaction create an opportunity for a truly responsive college classroom—one in which all students take responsibility for learning. Having mastered a basic, and yet cognitively sophisticated structure such as Think-Pair-Share, faculty are ready to move on to other structures suitable for higher education classrooms.

STRUCTURES SUITED FOR HIGHER EDUCATION CLASSROOMS

Roundtable

In this brainstorming technique students in a learning team, usually a quad or foursome, explore various aspects of a topic. The Roundtable procedure can be used to prevent two of the more common problems in small-group interaction, namely dominance by one individual and nonparticipation (also known as free-loading, hitchhiking, or coat-tailing). The Roundtable addresses these two problems by requiring turn-taking within the group.

The steps of the Roundtable are as follows: The teacher poses a question having multiple answers or gives each group a worksheet. The group has only one piece of paper or worksheet and perhaps only one pencil. A student writes down one response, says it aloud, and then passes the paper or worksheet to the person on the left. That person then writes down a response, says it aloud, and passes the paper to the left. The process continues until the allotted time—often as little as two minutes—expires. A student may choose to pass on one round and give an answer or response the next time. This activity builds positive interdependence among team members because of the shared writing surface, but more important, it builds team cohesion and reinforces the power of teamwork because students see in action the value of multiple viewpoints and ideas.

Some applications of the roundtable in diverse subject areas are as follows:

Mathematics: Write equations of pairs of parallel lines.

Science: List some of the most important scientific inventions of the past century.

Art History: Who are some of the greatest painters of the Renaissance?

Roundtable is valuable to review course material, to arrive at simple applications, to practice giving multiple responses, and most important, to creatively brainstorm ideas. It is not suitable for complex thinking and reasoning tasks that require group interaction and discussion. The main social skills needed to carry out the Roundtable are giving ideas, taking turns, listening without interrupting, and perhaps, encouraging. An oral version of the Roundtable, without writing on paper, is called a Roundrobin.

The Three-Step Interview

Common as an icebreaker or a team-building exercise, this structure also helps students reinforce and internalize important concept-related information based on lectures or textbook material. It can be used to share ideas such as hypotheses or reactions to a film or article. Some faculty have used it successfully as a modified role-playing activity, having students interview one another assuming the roles of historical characters. The interview questions, focused on content material and having no right or wrong solutions, are usually posed by the instructor. The three-step interview process makes a clear distinction between two roles: the listener (interviewer) and the speaker (interviewee). An interview differs from a conversation in that it is far more structured. The interviewer asks open questions and occasionally paraphrases but does not elaborate or share personal data. Students should be encouraged to draw information from their partners by asking probing questions and by requesting clarification or amplification. Hence, the main social skills used by the interviewer are listening respectfully, asking open questions, and paraphrasing.

The steps of the three-step interview process are as follows, with a group consisting of four members divided into two pairs: A and B, C and D. In Step 1, A interviews B while C interviews D; during Step 2 the partners reverse roles and B interviews A while D interviews C; in Step 3, the final one, a Roundrobin occurs with each person sharing information about his or her partner's responses in the group of four.

Applications for the three-step interview are numerous. It can be used at the beginning of a class for an icebreaker or for team building, with an interview question such as: Describe yourself in terms of your interests, hobbies, activities, favorite music, books, movies, sports, foods, family, or pets. Some professors prefer content-related questions that anchor the activity to the discipline and avoid a perception of frivolity. Thus, the interview is used most often to foster thinking about a particular academic topic. Some interview questions in varied subject areas include:

> *Mathematics:* Tell me what you know about different types of quadrilaterals.
>
> *Social Sciences:* If you were the President of the United States, what would you do to bring about peace in a particular area of the world, such as Bosnia. Why?
>
> *Theater:* What do you consider to be among the finest theatrical productions in the past year, and why?
>
> *Generic question prompts to structure interviews about a topic:* What interests you about ____? How can you use ____? Tell me what you know about ____. What information do you need about ____?

Depending on the amount of time allotted, more than one question can be asked. In any case, it is useful to add an additional question as a "sponge" activity to avoid off-task behavior or frustration for pairs finishing early, a recommended practice for many Cooperative Learning activities. The three-step interview also results in the formation of new learning quads, who may then move on to other cooperative activities. This structure reinforces listening and paraphrasing skills, helps students process and rehearse information, and results in shared insights.

Numbered Heads Together

This useful structure, described by Kagan (1992), is also known as a Problem Solving Lesson (Johnson, Johnson, & Smith, 1991) and in higher education as Structured Problem Solving (Cottell & Millis, 1993). Numbered Heads Together is used to combine small-group interaction with whole-class response. It can dramatically increase the number of students who are willing and able to respond successfully in the whole class. The steps of the numbered heads problem-solving procedure are as follows. Each student in a small group is given a number from one to four. The teacher poses a question, issue, or problem requiring higher-order thinking skills. Students talk this over within their group and prepare to respond. Students discuss the question or solve the problem, making certain that every group member can summarize the group's discussion or can explain the problem. The instructor calls a specific number and the designated team members (1, 2, 3, or 4) respond as group spokespersons. In higher education classrooms, playing cards can be used in place of numbers. Thus, teams will have an immediate identification (aces, deuces, etc.) and members can be called upon by the suit of the card (hearts, clubs, etc.).

Some applications of the structured problem-solving procedure are:

> *Geometry:* State possible values for the base and height of a set of rectangles that all have the same given area;   ·
>
> *Physiology:* Draw and label the bones in a human being's arms and legs;
>
> *Psychology:* What are some characteristics of a fully functioning person?;
>
> *Literature:* Explicate "I Am the Darker Brother" by Langston Hughes.

In this activity, students benefit from the verbalization, from the opportunity to exchange differing perspectives, and from the peer coaching that helps high and low achievers, alike. Less class time is wasted, as in Think-Pair-Share, on inappropriate responses, and the principle of simultaneity is operative because at any given time 25 percent of the students are vocal within their groups. Students become actively involved with the material. Since no one knows which number the teacher will call, each student has a vested interest in being able to articulate the appropriate response. Those chosen randomly as spokespersons—frequently students who do not volunteer during a whole-class discussion—feel far less threatened giving a team, rather than an individual, answer. Numbered Heads can be used for recall of information, creative thinking, and tasks requiring problem solving and reasoning. The main social skills involved are exchanging ideas, checking for understanding, explaining, and problem solving.

Pairs-Check

The Pairs-check procedure (Kagan, 1992) is used for practice and mastery of skills or procedures. Students work in pairs within their teams using two roles: performer (or solver) and coach. One person in the pair performs the task (e.g., solves a problem). The second person in the pair functions as a coach by observing carefully, giving feedback to the performer, and giving positive acknowledgment to the performer. Partners switch roles for the second performance or problem in the set. Then, the two pairs check their responses to the first two problems to see if they agree.

> Sample applications for the Pairs-check procedure are:
> *Mathematics:* Find the greatest common factor of two whole numbers;
> *Musical performance:* Play a two-octave D minor scale up and down;
> *Accounting:* List four controls for unreliability in a computer accounting system.

The main social skills for the coach in the pairs-check procedure are observing carefully; giving feedback by asking questions, pointing out errors, or giving hints; and giving positive acknowledgment to the performer.

Send/Pass a Problem

This structure, which was created in this version by the Howard County Maryland Staff Development Center, is particularly effective for problem solving and for building critical thinking skills. Teams identify the particular problem or issue upon which they wish to focus initially and write it down on the front of a folder or envelope. These issues can either be generated by students through an activity such as a Roundtable or can be selected by the teacher. Each team selects a different problem.

The process proceeds as follows. *Step 1:* each team brainstorms effective solutions for their chosen problem. At a predetermined time, the ideas are placed in the folder or envelope and forwarded to another team. *Step 2:* the members of the second team, without looking at the ideas already generated, compile their own list of solutions and place it in the folder. *Step 3:* this second set of ideas is forwarded to a third team, which now looks at the suggestions provided from the other teams, adds its own, and then decides on the two most effective solutions.

Besides encouraging collaborative higher-order thinking skills, this structure results in student evaluative judgments, the highest cognitive level in Bloom's well-known taxonomy. Reports to the whole group occur as time permits and can take many forms, including written reports when the material is relatively complex. Some faculty members use this structure for examination review sessions by putting typical exam questions in folders for group problem solving.

Applications in various disciplines are:

Sociology: Solutions to homelessness in major urban cities;

Literature: Creative written conclusions to brief, unfinished narratives;

Mathematics: Steps in solving complex problems having several approaches.

Fairly sophisticated structures such as Send-a-Problem promote the critical thinking skills that need to be nurtured and developed to produce citizens capable of functioning in an increasingly complex, technological society where the knowledge base is exploding at a phenomenal rate. Increasingly, cognitive researchers are recognizing that knowledge lies not solely in someone's head, but in socially shared activities and the interactions that occur with other people in the surrounding environment. Thus, work in groups can provide positive triggers to critical thinking. Many structures, such as Structured Controversy (Johnson, Johnson, & Smith, 1991; Johnson & Johnson, 1987) effectively promote critical thinking skills as students confront alternative viewpoints. Two structures that are particularly valuable in this regard are Jigsaw and Dyadic Essay Confrontations.

TWO STRUCTURES TO PROMOTE CRITICAL THINKING

Cooperative Learning structures enable faculty members to use the content of their own disciplines, resulting in situated learning where thinking skills develop within the context of the subject matter students are mastering (Davidson & Worsham, 1992). A recent review of the research literature on long-term retention of classroom-taught content (Semb & Ellis, 1994) suggests that classroom approaches, including peer tutoring, that "involve actively engaging learners in an enriched contextualized learning environment . . . should result in differential retention by making it easier for students to assimilate new information into existing memory structures or to create new well-organized ones" (p. 278).

Thus, faculty members who care deeply about student learning will want to move toward cooperative structures that promote higher-order thinking—playfully abbreviated as HOT in the K-12 literature—and depth of knowledge. Newmann and Wehlage (1993) describe development of such thinking skills in these words:

> Higher-order thinking (HOT) requires students to manipulate information and ideas in ways that transform their meaning and implications, such as when students combine facts and ideas in order to synthesize, generalize, explain, hypothesize, or arrive at some conclusion or interpretation. Manipulating information and ideas

through these processes allows students to solve problems and discover new (for them) meanings and understandings. When students engage in HOT, an element of uncertainty is introduced, and instructional outcomes are not always predictable. (p. 9)

Such higher-order thinking can occur when faculty members deliberately structure tasks to capitalize on student peer coaching and when, as Brookfield (1987) and Kurfiss (1988) suggest, they deliberately place students in situations where they encounter the alternative viewpoints that challenge existing beliefs and assumptions. The Jigsaw structure accomplishes these aims.

Jigsaw

In the Jigsaw structure, each member of the structured learning team assumes responsibility for a specific part of a problem or issue. In other words, each team member is responsible for a piece of the "puzzle." They are responsible not just for mastering or knowing their part; as "specialists," they must also be able to teach it to their fellow teammates. The steps of the Jigsaw procedure are the following:

1. Task Division: A task or passage of text material is divided into several component parts or topics.
2. Home Groups or Teams: Each group member volunteers to become an "expert" on a particular topic, one-fourth of the "puzzle" if there are four team members. Students can also be assigned to an expert team based on the numbers or suits assigned in Numbered Heads. If the original structured team consists of five members rather than four, then two students pair and work as a unit in their focus team and when they return to their original team.
3. Expert or Focus Groups: Students who have the same topics meet in expert groups to discuss the topics, master them, and plan how to teach them. Students thus have a two-tier assignment: they must master their fourth of the material and they must discover the best way to help others in their home team learn it. Students should be encouraged to think creatively about their approach by rehearsing their presentation and by designing visual aids or study sheets. Because teams larger than six become unwieldy, in large classes several expert teams can

work on the same piece of the assignment.

4. Home Groups or Teams: Students return to their original groups and teach what they have learned to their group members.
5. Quiz (optional): The quiz is taken individually.
6. Team Recognition (optional): Individual quiz scores are formed into team scores using an improvement score system; teams that meet criteria are publicly recognized in a class newsletter or other display.

When Steps 5 and 6 are used, the method is known as Jigsaw II (Slavin, 1986).

Applications of the Jigsaw procedure are:

Calculus: Sketching graphs of four different cubic polynomials;

Literature: Team members take a different character in a novel for an in-depth analysis;

Anthropology: Discussion of the major religious beliefs, kinship system, economic practices, and governance structure of a primitive society.

Jigsaw, as Clarke (1994) notes, was initially developed by a team of teachers, administrators, and researchers to create equal opportunities for participation and achievement in desegregated classrooms. Many versions of Jigsaw have been developed since Aronson, Blaney, Stephan, Sikes, and Snapp (1978) first published their work.

The value of Jigsaw lies in the teaching and peer-coaching process. Gere (1987), in speaking of the power of writing groups, emphasizes that

"The peer who says "I don't understand" establishes—more powerfully than any theory, instructor's exhortation, or written comment can—the "otherness" of the audience and pushes writers to respond to this otherness by more effective ways to convey ideas. . . . Participants in collaborative groups learn when they challenge one another with questions, when they use the evidence and information available to them, when they develop relationships among issues, when they evaluate their own thinking. In other words, they learn when they assume that knowledge is something they can help create rather than something to be received whole from someone else. (pp. 68-69)

Webb (1983, 1991) has found that giving detailed, elaborate explanations increases student achievement.

Jigsaw reinforces the most basic tenets of Cooperative Learning. Positive interdependence is fostered by the fact that students must work together and teach one another in order to get the "big picture," all of the information and skills they will need to solve the problem or in some disciplines, to function effectively on the job. At the same time, individual accountability is reinforced by the fact that students must learn all the information, not just their own portion, because they are tested individually. The fact that students interact within two different groups reinforces the idea of heterogeneity as a way to bring multiple perspectives to a given problem. The positive interactions that result from these brief, but intense encounters in the expert or focus groups help to develop the skills students will need in the "real world." The fact that expert teams have the responsibility of making certain that all members can successfully teach the materials/conclusions also reinforces the important concept of group processing and accountability. The collaborative exchanges also build critical thinking skills.

Dyadic Essay Confrontations (DEC)

In addition to building students critical thinking skills, Dyadic Essay Confrontations (DEC) allows instructors to incorporate meaningful writing assignments in their courses. Probably its most important use is to ensure that students read and understand the assigned reading material, thereby freeing class time for mastery and processing activities. Developed by Sherman (1991), in DEC, the instructor assigns readings such as a chapter from the course text, or a chapter complemented by primary sources or other selected readings. Sherman in (Millis, Cottell, & Sherman, 1993) states, "As originally conceived, this highly structured cooperative learning technique grew out of three concerns: (a) the need for students to encounter from classmates diverse opinions and unique perspectives on the required readings; (b) their need for meaningful integrative experiences to connect differing text materials;

(c) my desire—and certainly theirs!—for a more active and dynamic classroom environment," p. 12.

The DEC proceeds through a series of steps. Students are responsible outside of class for the following: (1) reading and reflecting on the assigned material; (2) formulating an integrative essay question, one that encourages comparisons between the current material and material previously covered; (3) preparing a model response to their own question, which is no longer than one-page, single-spaced; (4) bringing to class a copy of their essay question and, on a separate page, their model answer.

During class time, students are responsible for the following: (5) exchanging essay questions with the student with whom they are randomly paired; (6) writing a spontaneous essay in response to the question they receive from their partner; (7) reading and commenting on both the model answer to the question they received and on the spontaneous answer provided by a classmate to the essay question they formulated, looking in each case for divergent and convergent ideas; and (8) participating—if time permits—in a general discussion of the topic.

DEC can be used as an ongoing assignment over the course of a semester to ensure mastery of the course material. Students who have read and written two essays on each chapter in an ongoing series retain far more material than those who have merely heard a lecturer expound on them. As should be obvious, a complex, and yet highly focused, structure such as DEC has enormous value for university teaching and learning. With the virtue of versatility, it can promote higher-order thinking skills; focus students on outside assignments so that time is available for interactive group work rather than for lectures designed to cover the content; foster student-student interdependence, resulting in respect for diverse opinions; and reinforce the value of peer learning. It also complements writing across the curriculum efforts.

DEC can be used in virtually any discipline. Instructors in three different disciplines—psychology, English, and accounting—have effectively adopted the DEC structure to their university classes (Millis, Cottell, & Sherman, 1993).

Sherman uses it in educational psychology classes focused on social and developmental psychology theories. To evaluate the essays, he uses a combination of peer and instructor evaluation, assessing both the questions and the answers on the basis of five attributes: (1) an overall general impression; (2) importance; (3) clarity; (4) integration; and (5) creativity. He and the students use a five-point scale ranging from 0 (poor) to 4 (excellent) to rate each of the five attributes. They then evaluate the question and both answers—the out-of-class carefully prepared answer and the in-class spontaneous answer—using these criteria and scales. The total possible score is 120 (4 possible points for each of the five attributes as rated by the instructor and the peer/student evaluator).

In Modern Children's Literature, an upper-level English elective in an adult education setting, Millis must cover an enormous amount of content, packaged in a huge but readable text organized around eight different genres. The DEC process gives students learning incentives. She prefers to grade DEC-generated essays by emphasizing responses rather than grades. She thus uses a criterion-referenced grading scheme combined with mastery learning, allowing her to write frequent comments on student work, without, however, having to attach a specific grade to each piece. Ten points for each essay, the one prepared at home and the one written in class—if they are of sufficient depth and quality—count toward the total number of points students acquire for the course grade.

Cottell uses DEC in two accounting courses, an honors seminar focused on accounting ethics and an advanced financial accounting seminar offered as an elective to masters of accounting students. In the latter course, the primary texts are FASB Discussion Memoranda, which present alternative points of view on recommended accounting treatments of issues currently before the Financial Accounting Standards Board (FASB). Each day students read a portion of the FASB Discussion Memorandum and write a question and response about that section. In this class the DEC essays are not individually graded: the class grade is based solely on a paper on the accounting issues addressed by the FASB Discussion Memoranda.

Conclusion

All educators are aware of the cries for educational reform and of the challenges facing higher education and society in general. Ekroth (1990) says "Today's professors are challenged to teach a student population increasingly diverse in age, levels of academic preparation, styles of learning, and cultural background. Professors are now expected not only to 'cover the material,' but also to help students to think critically, write skillfully, and speak competently" (p. 1). Cooperative Learning addresses many of these issues. Johnson and Johnson (1989) note, for example, that "Cooperative learning is indicated whenever the learning goals are highly important, the task is complex or conceptual, problem solving is desired, divergent thinking or creativity is desired, quality of performance is expected, higher-order reasoning strategies and critical thinking are needed, and long-term retention is desired" (p. 13). Given the validity of this statement, it is difficult to envision an academic setting where Cooperative Learning would not prove beneficial. Because the structures enable instructors to adopt and adapt cooperative techniques, more and more faculty members are embracing a more enlightened view of teaching that emphasizes cooperation and positive interactions.

REFERENCES

Aronson, E., Blaney, N., Stephan, C., Sikes, J., & Snapp, M. (1978). *The Jigsaw Classroom.* Beverly Hills, CA: Sage, Publications, Inc.

Astin, A.W. (1993). *What Matters in College: Four Critical Years Revisited.* San Francisco, CA: Jossey-Bass.

Brookfield, S. D. (1987). *Developing Critical Thinkers: Challenging Adults to Explore Alternative Ways of Thinking and Acting.* San Francisco: Jossey-Bass.

Clarke, J. (1994). "Pieces of the Puzzle: The Jigsaw Method." In Sharan, S., ed. *Handbook of Cooperative Learning Methods.* Westport, CT: Greenwood Press.

Cottell, P. G., Jr., & Millis, B. J. (1993). *Instructor's Resource Guide for Financial Accounting: Information for Decisions.* Cincinnati, OH: South-Western.

Davidson, N., & Worsham, T., eds. (1992). *Enhancing Thinking through Cooperative Learning.* New York: Teachers College Press.

Ekroth, L. (1990). "Why Professors Don't Change." In L. Ekroth, ed. *Teaching Excellence: Toward the Best in the Academy* (Winter-Spring). Stillwater, OK: Professional and Organizational Development Network in Higher Education.

Gere, A. R. (1987). *Writing Groups: History, Theory, and Implications.* Carbondale and Edwardsville: Southern Illinois University Press.

Johnson, D. W., & Johnson, R. T. (1987). *Creative Conflict.* Edina, MN: Interaction Book Company.

———. (1989). *Leading the Cooperative School.* Edina, MN: Interaction Book Company.

Johnson, D. W., Johnson, R. T., & Smith, K. (1991). *Active Learning: Cooperation in the College Classroom.* Edina, MN: Interaction Book Company.

Kagan, S. (1992). *Cooperative Learning.* San Juan Capistrano, CA: Resources for Teachers.

Kurfiss, J. G. (1988). *Critical Thinking: Theory, Research, Practice, and Possibilities.* ASHE-ERIC Higher Education Report No. 2. Washington, D. C.: Association for the Study of Higher Education.

Lyman, F. T. (1992). "Think-Pair-Share, Thinktrix, Thinklinks, and Weird Facts: An Interactive System for Cooperative Thinking." In N. Davidson & T. Worsham, eds. *Enhancing Thinking through Cooperative Learning.* New York: Teachers College Press.

Millis, B. J., Cottell, P., & Sherman, L. (Spring 1993). Stacking the DEC to promote critical thinking: Applications in three disciplines. *Cooperative Learning and College Teaching* 3(3): 12-14.

Newmann, F. M., & Wehlage, G. G. (April 1993). Five standards for authentic instruction. *Educational Leadership* 50(7): 8-12.

Semb, G. B., & Ellis, J. A. (Summer 1994). Knowledge taught in school: What is remembered? *Review of Educational Research* 64(2): 253-86.

Sherman, L. W. (April 1991). "Cooperative Learning in Post Secondary Education: Implications from Social Psychology for Active Learning Experiences." Presentation at the American Educational Research Association, Chicago, IL.

Slavin, R. E. (1986). *Using Student Team Learning: The Johns Hopkins Team Learning Project.* Baltimore, MD: The Johns Hopkins University Press.

———. (1993). What can post-secondary cooperative learning learn from elementary and secondary research? *Cooperative Learning and College Teaching* 4(1): 2-3.

Smith, K. A., Johnson, D. W., & Johnson, R. T. (1992). "Cooperative Learning and Positive Change in Higher Education." In A. Goodsell, M. Mahler, V. Tinto, B. L. Smith, & J. MacGregor, eds. *Collaborative Learning: A Sourcebook for Higher Education,* 34-36. University Park, PA: National Center on Postsecondary Teaching, Learning, and Assessment.

Webb, N. (1983). Predicting learning from student interaction: Defining the interaction variable. *Educational Psychologist* 18: 33-41.

————. Task-related verbal interaction and mathematics learning in small groups. *Journal of Research in Mathematics Education* 22: 366-89.

15

THINK-PAIR-SHARE AND THE GRADUATE TEACHING ASSISTANT

by Douglas C. Foyle

Instructors of large lecture classes often face the common problem of individually engaging students. At many universities, lecture classes with enrollments of 250, and even up to 600 students, are not uncommon. In this environment, where anonymity is the rule rather than the exception, much of the learning experience is passive, with students attending lectures, listening, and taking notes, but rarely interacting with the professor and/or other students. In an attempt to increase interaction, schools usually require students in these lecture classes to attend weekly discussion sections (led by a teaching assistant) to discuss the course material. In theory, these sections allow students to debate course material, to test out new ideas, to extend the concepts introduced in lecture and readings, to challenge their fellow students' ideas, and to be challenged in return.

Unfortunately, discussion sections often suffer from the very shortcomings they are intended to alleviate. The following observations are based on my experiences as a Stanford University undergraduate student and as a graduate teaching assistant and instructor at Duke University.

First, in a discussion section, passive learning often continues for a large percentage of the students. In sections that regularly contain at least 20 (and often approach 30) students, a relatively small number of students (5-8) tend to become verbally involved in the discussion. The other students continue to attend, listen, and take notes, as during lectures, unless directly prompted. When the teaching assistant directly questions these passive participators, they tend to respond with short, poorly developed answers, and seem to experience a certain degree of discomfort. The discomfort seems to be about the act of speaking in section, rather than a failure to do the required readings.

Second, the "fear of being wrong" also seems to pervade these sections. Because discussion sections are designed to induce debate, students sometimes seem to feel uncomfortable either challenging other students or being challenged themselves. Because students are, by the nature of the classroom experience, learning the material, they are understandably less confident in their viewpoints and assessments than they might be otherwise. In addition, a discussion grade, often assigned by the teaching assistant based on the quality of an individual's interactions in the section, serves to enhance the potential evaluation anxiety. These dynamics tend to encourage passive observation, rather than active participation.

Third, some students' mental processes are faster than others in the formulation of responses (quite apart from their intelligence or preparation for section). As a result, certain individuals may dominate discussion, not because of the higher quality of their insights, but because they can more quickly formulate a response that they would like to share with the group.

Fourth, the students' lack of familiarity with each other may also detract from the quality of discussion, especially when discussion section meets only once a week. Students rarely have the opportunity to get to know and become comfortable with the other students in the section. This situation can work to inhibit a free-flowing discussion and it also exacerbates the three previously identified problems of discussion sections.

All teachers face the same challenges to engage students, activate their minds, and provoke stimulating and educational discussions. The Cooperative Learning technique known as Think-Pair-Share (TPS) can contribute to the achievement of these goals (Lyman, 1981, 1987, 1988, 1992). The TPS teaching strategy begins with the instructor assigning each student a partner. Then, the instructor poses a question to the entire section that will become the basis for discussion (such as "What foreign policy orientation should the United States adopt in the current international environment: isolationist or internationalist? Why?") The instructor then allows a short period of time for the students to individually reflect on the question and formulate how they would answer the question. For college students, I allowed a "Think" period of about 5 seconds. Upon an indication from the instructor, the students discuss their views with their partners. During this "Pair" discussion, the instructor should move about the room and monitor the interactions between the pairs of students. This period lasts between two and five minutes depending on the vitality of the individual discussions. Finally, during the "Share" period, the instructor facilitates a discussion of the question with the entire section. This process can be repeated a number of times in a single class period with a new partner for each discussion question.

The TPS technique can contribute to learning in a number of ways. First, TPS can promote more widespread involvement in discussion. In my experience using TPS, I found that more students took an active part in discussion. Second, TPS fosters a learning environment that allows students to deal with material in a less intimidating atmosphere. Third, by allowing a "'Think" period, the wait-time is increased, which provides slower processing thinkers the time to formulate and organize their thoughts in preparation for participation in discussion. Fourth, through the pair discussions, students can become familiar with the other students in the classroom. While students may come to know each other over the many weeks of the course, the pairing technique can accelerate this process. Fifth, by discussing their views with a partner before the larger discussion, students can gain confidence in their own views, which increases the likelihood of verbal participation in discussion.

I reached the above conclusions regarding the utility of TPS based on my observations and experiences with the strategy in two discussion sections of a large lecture class at Duke University. The interdisciplinary course entitled Contemporary Global Issues was intended for intermediate level students from the fields of political science, history, anthropology, sociology, and area studies and included students majoring in fields as varying as English, biology, and electrical engineering.

Because of the interdisciplinary nature of the course, many students did not feel completely comfortable with the new material. The course held a total enrollment of approximately 260 students. The full class met twice weekly for lecture and once weekly in smaller discussion sections. The discussion sections contained 26 students, on average, most of whom did not previously know each other.

To determine the usefulness of TPS in this environment, I applied it in five different instructional conditions during the course. The following paragraphs are a report of my observations of TPS's effect, in each instructional condition, on discussion and the students and my brief comparisons to my experiences as a teaching assistant for the same class when I did not use TPS.

TPS for the Full Class Period

At the first section meeting, I used TPS during the entire class period, as described above, and found that TPS enhanced the discussion in these sections. As a whole, the paired discussions progressed quite well with both partners contributing ideas to the conversation. In my monitoring of discussions, I overheard many interesting and insightful comments. In addition, the full section discussion proved quite fruitful, with most students contributing to the discussion. I found the students to be fairly unrestrained in their comments and discussion flowed freely. Switching partners also seemed to allow the students to familiarize themselves quickly with their fellow students.

Partial TPS Use

In another session, I started discussion without using the TPS technique. I noticed immediately a marked decrease in both the amount of discussion and the number of people participating in class as compared to the previous section. About midway through the session, I again began using the TPS technique. In the pairs, I noticed the interesting and broad-ranging discussions I had witnessed in the previous section. During group discussions, while the level of participation did not reach that of the class using TPS for the full period, more students participated in the group discussion during the TPS part of the discussion than when I had not used TPS.

Traditional Discussion Section

In a later session in the same course, I did not employ TPS at any point in the section. I found that discussion was more difficult to get started between the students than when TPS had been used with the same group of students. In addition, a few individuals tended to dominate discussion. The group interactions seemed less free-flowing than after the use of TPS and students were slower in their responses to questions presented for discussion. Finally, some individuals, who had actively participated in the group discussion when using TPS, failed to take part in the group discussion.

TPS As Discussion Foundation

I used an adapted version of TPS to have the students investigate certain foreign policy paradigms and the implications of these views. After using TPS as a method to establish a basis of knowledge for the students, I led the section in a discussion of a new issue to examine the transfer of learning effects. I found that discussion remained animated and active, which seems to imply that TPS could be used successfully to introduce students to a new topic. I surmised that TPS built the confidence of the students in their knowledge on the general subject matter and made them more comfortable in discussing related issues.

Modified TPS—Large Group

I divided the section into three separate groups and assigned each group a different discussion topic and then moved about the room and monitored the group deliberations to ensure that the conversations were proceeding on track. I found that lively and insightful exchanges occurred within the groups. I also noticed that not all individuals spoke during these group discussions. Following these group discussions, the class came together and discussed the three separate viewpoints as a whole. Interestingly, I found that some of the people who had not participated in the small-group discussions did participate in the full class discussion. I concluded that the group discussion served the purpose of building the confidence of these students, which led them to take a more active role in the large-group discussion than they had in the small-group discussion.

One anecdote reveals the general benefit that TPS can have for both the student and the teaching assistant or instructor in the evaluation of student performance. Early in the term, one student approached me after section and expressed the concern that he was not participating fully in the large-group discussion. Because the subject matter was not this individual's area of expertise, he felt intimidated in the large discussion due to the fact that he had never had a class that covered similar material (as some of the other students had). Using TPS, I had observed him in the pair discussions making some truly perceptive comments. Given this knowledge, I was able to speak to the student about his abilities and concerns and to assure him that his discussion performance was fine. TPS allowed me to support the student and increase his confidence, because I could give him direct and immediate feedback as to his abilities. While this student never became one of the most active participants in discussion, I did notice that he participated more often in subsequent group discussions.

Despite my positive experience with TPS at the university level, there is one caveat. A possible barrier to implementating any of the TPS modes is the student's initial resistance to the technique. This initial resistance was likely due to the fact that TPS represented a new mode of interaction to all of the students. The students seemed uncomfortable with TPS itself, presumably because the method fell outside of their "normal" section experience. Students initially seemed uncertain about the process; however, they quickly became comfortable with the method once they had gained some experience with it.

In summary, I found it enlightening to compare my experiences with discussion sections in which I used TPS with my experiences during the previous year when I was a teaching assistant for the same class but was as yet unfamiliar with TPS. First, I found that student interactions were more collegial during the term I employed TPS. The students seemed more comfortable in the classroom, suggesting that the students felt more confidence in themselves and trust in others. Second, I noticed a marked increase in the level of participation in discussion when TPS was used. As a rough estimate, approximately 80 percent of the students participated in the group discussions after using TPS. This compares with the previous year where the number of students continually participating in discussion (without being specifically prompted) ranged between 33 percent and 50 percent.

Finally, the most common fear among teaching assistants is that they will attempt to lead a discussion only to discover that no one is following them. In essence, the worst nightmare of many section leaders is that discussion will consist of questions by the teaching assistant and either short, tentative responses from the students or, at worst, prolonged silence. TPS can address this concern. During the year that I did not use TPS, I sometimes found starting a discussion a daunting task. After introducing a discussion topic, one or two students would comment, then discussion would quickly die down. With TPS, a constant and consistent result across all TPS conditions was a vibrant discussion.

In my experience, Think-Pair-Share provides a method to avoid a number of potential discussion section problems. Once students are given the time to organize their thoughts and discuss them with a partner, they were much more likely to contribute to subsequent group discussions. In sum, Think-Pair-Share provides instructors and graduate assistants, teaching in a number of institutional environments, a strategy to enhance both student learning and the instructor's ability to promote an active and stimulating classroom discussion.

REFERENCES

Lyman, F. (1981). "The Responsive Classroom Discussion." In A. S. Anderson, ed. *Mainstreaming Digest*. College Park, MD: College of Education, University of Maryland.

————. (1987). Think-Pair-Share: An expanding teaching technique. *MAACIE Cooperative News* 1(1): 1-2.

Lyman, F. T., Jr. (1988). "Think Pair Share." (A Lifelong Learning 14-minute videotape produced by The Howard County Public School System and the University of Maryland). Distributed by the NEA Professional Library, P.O. Box 509, West Haven, CT 06516-0509.

————. (1992). "Think-Pair-Share, Thinktrix, Thinklinks, and Weird Facts: An Interactive System for Cooperative Learning." In N. Davidson & T. Worsham, ed. *Enhancing Thinking through Cooperative Learning*. New York: Teachers College Press, 169-81.

SELECTED RESOURCES

Cooper, J., ed. *Cooperative Learning and College Teaching*. (A Newsletter.) The Network for Cooperative: Learning in Higher Education, New Forums Press, Inc., P.O. Box 876, Stillwater, OK 74076.

Cooper J., Prescott, S., Cook, L., Smith, L., & Cuseo, J. (1989). *Cooperative Learning and College Instruction: Effective Use of Student Learning Teams*. Center for Quality Education. 1000 Carson, CA.

Goodsell, A., Maher, M., Tinto, V., Smith, B., & Macgregor, J. (1992).*Collaborative Learning: A Sourcebook for Higher Education*. National Center on Postsecondary Teaching, Learning, and Assessment, The Pennsylvania State University, 403 South Allen Street, Suite 104, University Park, PA 16801-5252.

Graves, N., ed. *Cooperative Learning, The Magazine for Cooperation in Education*. Box 1582, Santa Cruz, CA 95061-1582.

> *Thematic issues:*
> Cooperative Learning: A Resource Guide, 1990 edition. (September 1990). Volume 11, Number 1.
> Cooperative Learning 101: Applications in Higher Education. (Spring, 1993). Volume 13, Number 3.
> 1993 Resource Guide. (Special Issue). Volume 12, Number 4.

Johnson, R., Johnson, D., & Smith, K. (1991). *Active Learning: Cooperation in the Classroom*. Interaction Book Co., 7208 Cornelia Drive, Edina, MN 55435.

Johnson, D. W., Johnson, R. T., & Smith, K. A. (1991). *Cooperative Learning: Increasing College Faculty Instructional Productivity*. ASHE-ERIC Higher Education Report 91-4, The George Washington University, School of Education and Human Development, One Dupont Circle, Suite 630, Washington, DC 20036-1183.

Landa, A., & Tarule, J.M., eds. (1992). *Models II: Collaboration in Postsecondary Education*. Collaborative Learning Project, Lesley College, 29 Everett Street, Cambridge, MA 02138-2790.

Lyman, L., & Foyle, H. C. (1990). *Cooperative Grouping for Interactive Learning: Students, Teachers, and Administrators*. Washington, DC: National Education Association.

Meyers, C., & Jones, T. (1993). *Promoting Active Learning: Strategies for the College Classroom*. Jossey-Bass, Inc., Publishers, 350 Sansome Street, San Francisco, CA 94104.

THE AUTHORS

Tara S. Azwell (Ph.D., Kansas State University, 1989) teaches in the elementary education area of the Teacher Education Division of the Teachers College, Emporia State University (KS). She is co-author of the National Education Association book, *Cooperative Learning in the Elementary Classroom* (1993).

Neil Davidson (Ph.D., University of Wisconsin-Madison, 1970) is a past president of the International Association for the Study of Cooperation in Education (IASCE). He is a professor in the Department of Curriculum and Instruction, College of Education, University of Maryland, College Park, Maryland.

David C. Foyle (Ph. D., Indiana University, 1981) is a research scientist in the Aerospace Human Factors Research Division at NASA Ames Research Center, Moffett Field, California. His interests include the study of pilot use of aircraft instrumentation and the design of advanced avionics displays.

Douglas C. Foyle (Ph.D. candidate in Political Science at Duke University) specializes in international relations and American foreign policy.

Peter Frederick (Ph.D., University of California-Berkeley, 1966) teaches American History, African-American History, American-Indian Culture and History, and social science methods at Wabash College (IN). He is co-author of *The American People* (Harper-Collins) and author of *Knights of the Golden Rule* (University of Kentucky).

Carol B. Furtwengler (Ph.D., George Peabody College of Vanderbilt University, 1980) is an associate professor in the Department of Educational Administration and Supervision at The Wichita State University (KS).

Scott Irwin (Ph.D., The University of Texas at Austin, 1970) is a science methods professor who teaches in the elementary education program in The Teachers College, Emporia State University (KS).

Joanne M. Larson (Ph.D., University of North Dakota, 1993) is an assistant professor in the Division of Teacher Education at Emporia State University (KS). She teaches courses in reading education and her research interests include the connections between theory and practice and reading in the secondary schools.

Frank T. Lyman, Jr. (Ph.D., University of Maryland, 1978) is a Professional Development School Center Coordinator for the University of Maryland–Howard County Schools. He specializes in educational solution finding in education and teacher education. He is the developer of the cooperative learning strategy called Think-Pair-Share.

Lawrence Lyman (Ph.D., Kansas State University, 1984) has served as an elementary school teacher and principal. He currently is a professor in the Teacher Education division of The Teachers College, Emporia State University (KS). He has co-authored several books on Cooperative Learning for the National Education Association.

Teresa A. Mehring (Ph.D., University of Kansas, 1981) is the Associate Dean of The Teachers College, Emporia State University (KS). She is a member of the Psychology and Special Education division in which she teaches educational psychology and related courses.

Barbara J. Millis (Ph.D., Florida State University, 1981), Assistant Dean, Faculty Development, University of Maryland University College, has been using cooperative learning techniques in her literature classes and during frequent workshops and presentations at professional conferences and institutions of higher education. She has published numerous articles on all aspects of faculty development, including "Helping Faculty Build Learning Communities through Cooperative Groups," "Fulfilling the Promise of the 'Seven Principles' Through Cooperative Learning," "Enhancing Adult Learning Through Cooperative Small Groups," and "Cooperative Learning in Accounting."

Jean Morrow, OSM, (Ed.D., Boston University, 1989) is a former elementary teacher and secondary principal. She taught mathematics education in The Teachers College of Emporia State University (KS). Currently, she is the director of the university's Professional Development School in Olathe, Kansas.

William G. Samuelson (Ph.D., University of Texas at Austin, 1967) is a professor of curriculum and instruction in The Teachers College, Emporia State University (KS). He specializes in the philosophy and history of American education and also teaches secondary methods courses.

Connie S. Schrock (Ph.D., Kansas State University, 1989) is a mathematics professor in the College of Liberal Arts & Sciences of Emporia State University (KS). She also instructs secondary mathematics preservice teachers.

Michael G. Shafto (Ph. D., Princeton University, 1974) is the Assistant Division Chief for Research in the Aerospace Human Factors Research Division at NASA Ames Research Center, Moffett Field, California. His interests include the study of human-computer interaction and the human factors of intelligent computer systems.

Laura M. Ventimiglia (M. Ed., Northeastern University, 1990) is an instructor of psychology at North Shore Community College and a visiting lecturer at Salem State College (MA).

Bill Yates (Ph.D., University of Oregon, 1988) is Director of Educational Computing in The Teachers College, Emporia State University (KS).